MARKETING and PROMOTING your own SEMINARS and WORKSHOPS

by Fred Gleeck

"If you're averse to making money, this is not the book for you."

Marketing and Promoting
Your Own Seminars and Workshops
by Fred Gleeck

© 2001
Fred Gleeck
Fast Forward Press
1-800-FGLEECK (345-3325)
www.seminarexpert.com

Printed in the United States of America

Cover and text design: TLC Graphics, www.TLCGraphics.com

ISBN#: 0-936965-08-8

Contents

To collect your free gift (worth $77) send an email to tips@seminarexpert.com

To collect your free gift (worth $77) send an email to tips@seminarexpert.com

---

*P*reface

Who's this Gleeck Guy and Why Should I Listen to Him?

I only know how to do a few things really well in life. As a kid growing up in the Philippines I became the Junior Amateur Golf Champion. In college, I figured out a way to get really good grades. But when I got out into the "real world" after getting my Master's degree in international business, I kept getting fired. Not just once or twice! I was fired from five major Fortune 500 companies. In a row!

There seemed to be unanimous agreement that I should be self-employed. Back in 1984, I saw a guy named Howard Shenson (one of my mentors, now deceased), give a seminar on starting your own consulting business. I watched him and thought, "Not only can I do that, I can do that better than he can."

I had always wanted to get my degree in theatre. My parents told me they would pay for any amount of education I wanted to get, as long as it was in business. A more **practical** field, in my father's opinion. It turned out to be good counsel.

After getting fired for the fifth time and having seen Howard do his seminar, I put two and two together. I would do seminars on business topics for a living. This would combine my theatrical passion with my academic background in business.

So, on a nice sunny day in Saddlebrook, New Jersey, in 1984, I launched my seminar career. I gave my first "open to the public" seminar.

The title of that seminar was "Starting and Building Your Own Consulting Business." I gave this seminar **never having done a day of consulting** work in my life. I **don't** recommend you follow my lead on this one!

I had, however, read close to 70 books on the topic. I'm not exaggerating! I then synopsized them and created a seminar of my own. I found out later that I had a talent for taking a lot of complex information and delivering it in an easy-to-understand and logical fashion. People will actually pay you for this talent, I've since discovered!

So I got up that Saturday morning, drove a rental car from my apartment in New York City to the Saddlebrook Marriott. There I gave my first seminar. I made just over $2,000 net profit. Not only did I enjoy the money, but I had a hell of a good time. I decided that this was the way I wanted to make my living.

So, that's how this "story" starts.

If you want to, you can do the same. You **can** make a living doing seminars. And have a lot of fun in the process. Or you can do seminars to supplement your existing income.

The problem is this. You need a roadmap. I had a decent roadmap myself. In addition to his material on consulting, Howard Shenson also had developed a lot of information on doing your own seminars and workshops. I read them over and over again. I then looked for and discovered more information on the topic. I consumed everything I found!

I have now developed my own system for doing seminars. A system that works! It will work for you as well. But, I suggest that you carefully follow my instructions. I suggest you don't try "improvising" until you've done it my way for a while. If you don't follow this advice, you may lose a **lot** of money. The seminar game is a tricky one. Particularly if you're new to the game.

I have **never** lost money on a seminar that I promoted. Not many people that I know in this business can say the same.

In this book, I'm going to share my system with you. Not part of the system! The **whole** system. That's what you paid for and that's what you're going to get. I'm not going to hold anything back!

So fasten your seat belt and get out your highlighter! Here is where the fun begins.

Also, as a registered buyer of this book you're entitled to receive a half-hour of my time over the phone. Please take advantage of this bonus. It is worth a minimum of $350. (Yes, I'm proud to say that I charge that much for my time.)

I suggest you use this time wisely. Read this entire book. Take notes as you go. Send me an email with all of your questions. I'll set up a time for us to talk and get all of your questions answered. How's that for fair?

Now ... let's get going!

Who's This Book For?

I have only one objective with this book: to show you how to make a lot of money in the seminar business. If you're averse to making money, this is **not** the book for you.

I love to make money. I **hate** to spend it. I'm frugal. Others might use the word cheap. Everything except for my sweaters. (I'll tell you that story in a few pages.)

Many people have negative feelings about making money. They feel that you shouldn't try to get rich. I completely disagree. Even if you're out to "save the planet", why not make a bunch of money and then give it away to one of your favorite charities or causes? Mother Teresa was interviewed near the end of her illustrious life of helping the lepers of India. "People think I'm a poor nun," she said with a sly smile. "I'm actually running a multi-million dollar business. Helping people costs money!"

I read a book years ago by a guy named Jerry Gilies. He wrote a book called "Moneylove." If you can, pick up a copy of it. He talks about the difference between prosperity and poverty consciousness. It's out of print, but you might be able to find it at a used book store or on-line.

So if you're looking for all of the touchy, feely stuff, you've knocked on the wrong door.

Don't get me wrong, though. If you run your seminar business correctly you will behave in a highly ethical manner. Not only is that the **right** thing to do, it's in your own financial best interest to do so.

At the end of the day, this book has been written to show you how to make money, and a **lot** of it.

A Word of Caution

Whatever you do, do **not** skip to Chapter 17 before you read the whole book. I know you're tempted to do so, but resist the temptation! In that chapter, I summarize the most important points in this book and I don't want you to read those before you've read the intervening tens of thousands of words.

Seriously.

*I*ntroduction

What's Your Goal Doing These Events?

Why are you interested in giving seminars and workshops? Before you can either get very good at giving them or make much money from them, you have to be clear about your goals. Different people come to this business with different objectives in mind. The important question isn't so much what specific objective you have, but that you have a good reason for wanting to do something that is often as demanding as presenting and marketing seminars.

Here are some of the most common reasons people provide when asked whey they want to be in the seminar business:

Money. This is the number one reason people give seminars. And it's the one I'm focused on, both in this book and in my career. If you want to change the world, I'm all for it. But recognize that it will take money to change the world. Go get some money, then use it to change the world! There are two kinds of money in seminars: direct (seminar fees) and indirect (product sales and consulting assignments).

Desire to Share Knowledge. Some people do seminars regardless of whether they make money or not because they have some knowledge or experience they feel a need to share. That's a great and compelling motivation for doing seminars. But even people with this motivation can benefit from having a line of products backing up their seminar because not everyone learns the same way and not everyone can get to your seminars.

Fame. A few people see seminars as a way to become famous. I doubt that works very well. I think seminars are a part of a larger marketing plan that can, in totality, have the effect of making you famous. But fame doesn't come to people who **only** give seminars. At least not that I know about!

Seminar Business Pros and Cons

As you can probably tell, I LOVE the seminar business. It happens to fit all of my requirements in terms of the type of job that I like. Here's a list of the pros and cons about the seminar business.

Pros

It's your own business

Unless you choose to do seminar work for another company or individual, it's your business. You control it, you do what you want, you run it your way. For someone like me who doesn't particularly like others telling me what to do, this is a necessity of any business in which I'd get involved having.

You can make lots of money

With the right topic that's run correctly, the seminar business can be very lucrative. Many successful seminar promoters make millions of dollars a year. Others make a very good, high six figure income. If you're good, you won't have to worry about making big money.

You're always learning new things

If you're doing your homework in your field, you'll always be learning new stuff. If you aren't a continual learner, your seminar content will suffer.

You get to travel if you want

If you like to travel, you can rack up plenty of frequent flier miles. You can only give so many seminars in your own "home" market without reaching saturation. That means that you'll have to take your show on the road.

I have logged over 2,000,000 miles with American Airlines since I started doing seminars. I now try and do a lot of seminars in Las Vegas and have people come to me instead. It's a lot easier on my body not to have to travel continually.

You gain a lot of prestige

Like being an author, being a seminar leader will give you a lot of prestige. People look at seminar leaders like minor celebrities. If you're a Tony Robbins or someone else who does infomercials you

---

will be perceived as a demi-god by many adoring fans. If you like this adoration and praise, the seminar business will give it to you.

You meet interesting people

I have met some fascinating people in my travels through the seminar business. If you like people and are open to meeting them you'll meet plenty. Many will be intensely interesting. This is one ancillary benefit that really appeals to me.

You position yourself as the expert in your topic

Other than writing books, giving seminars is the ultimate way to position yourself as the expert in your field. You'll be very visible. Many people will see you. Potential clients will seek you out. You'll get press coverage. You'll be acknowledged as one of THE experts in your field.

You generate a lot of consulting work

My consulting model which I discuss in my book "Consulting Secrets to Triple Your Income" revolves around the concept of trading people up your funnel. Seminars are one very important element in your funnel system.

You get to be a ham

If you love getting up in front of people and having your own stage on which to perform, this is the business for you.

People to pay to be your prospects

If you charge for your seminars many people will show up, pay you money, buy your products and then turn around and hire you as a consultant. What a country! What a business. Consultants who spend their time running after potential clients are nuts. This is a much easier way.

You can record your seminars and get paid for them even when you're not doing them

You can make money by recording your seminars and then selling people the audio or video version of the event. What can be better? You do it once and then you get paid over and over.

Cons

Travel gets tiring

Like I said earlier, I have done a LOT of travel. Frankly, I'm now sick of it. Travel can and does take a toll on your body. I would now to prefer to do all of my work in my home city. I would then only travel for vacations. Unfortunately, this is tough to do if you're in the seminar business.

It can be an up and down business

If you're looking for a business that provides you with security, this isn't it. Money comes in very erratically. Some days you're swimming in it and other days there's nothing!

For this reason, it's imperative you do two things. First, develop products to smooth our your revenue curve. Secondly, put your money away when it's coming in.

It's energy draining: it's tough to do all the other stuff

If you do a seminar all day, you'll be dead tired by 8 o'clock. Don't think you can do this and something else the same day.

It can be very stressful

This is an understatement! There can be a lot of stress associated with this business. People not registering quickly, preparing all of the logistics, etc., etc.

Conclusion

To me, the pros vastly outweigh the cons. But, that's how I feel. You need to review the above items and make the choice for yourself. Most people who get into the seminar business find they love it!

Difference Between Seminars and Bootcamps

Seminars and bootcamps are different. Seminars are fairly didactic. The speakers talk and the participants listen. A seminar is generally a one-way rather than a conversation. This is primarily due to time constraints. Most seminars are either one or two days.

Although some may use the term differently, my definition of a bootcamp is a multi-day "seminar" which is much more interactive. Bootcamps generally have multiple speakers and often use more group exercise discussions.

Bootcamps usually go longer each day. A seminar is a more corporate term and people tend to think of them pretty generically. It refers to an event that runs during normal business hours.

That is definitely not true for bootcamps. Many of the bootcamps I have given and attended have gone from 12 to 14 hours each day.

One of the appeals of a bootcamp from a marketing standpoint is the volume of information you can show people that you'll be able to deliver. In fact, bootcamps are often a bit overwhelming for participants. Most people get pretty burned-out, regardless of the quality of the speakers, because of the sheer volume of information.

That doesn't mean I don't suggest you do them. If you do, though, you'll need to run your bootcamps with breaks for meals and even exercise (for those who believe in the concept).

Also, bootcamps are much more apt to have "hot seats." Seldom will you see hot seats used in the seminar business because there simply isn't enough time. (I discuss the hot seat concept in Chapter 9.)

Four Steps to Success in the Seminar Business

There are 4 steps to success in the seminar business.

First, you have to promote the seminar and get people into the room. Next, you have to give a great seminar. Then you have to get people to spend money at the seminar itself in the form of products. Then you have to get them to come back to other seminars and events you have. Then you have to get them to buy more from you. Finally, you have to get them to use you as a consultant and to tell everyone else about you and your services.

Simple, right? Well, not really! But, if you follow my roadmap it's possible. So keep reading!

Get people in the door

Getting people in the door is the job of marketing your seminar. No matter how great a seminar you've designed, it won't make a difference if you can't get people to walk through your doors and attend.

Give a Great Seminar

Once you get them to come through your doors you've got to exceed their expectations.

Get People to Buy Your Products

When people come to your seminars, you have to learn how to sell products from the platform. If you don't like this, you're in the wrong business. I'll show you how to do it right.

After they leave your seminar, get them to come back to other seminars and buy other products

If people come to your event and are delighted, they will come back to other events that you do.

Get them to use you as a consultant

If you're good at all of the above, they'll use you as a consultant. It will take little if any marketing.

Your Database: Your Most Important Asset

One of my two or three biggest mistakes in the seminar business (early on) revolved around the issue of my database. For the first few years, I didn't keep one. This was an incredibly stupid mistake on my part. Please don't make the same mistake.

You need to create two databases. One should be a "regular" database (physical address) and the other should be an email database.

Not only do you need to capture the names and email addresses of your attendees, you need to mail to them on a regular basis. You also need to send them a physical "snail mail" piece a minimum of 4 times a year. If you don't mail to your names that often, they will get stale. Their response rate of any offer you make will suffer.

For your email list you need to mail to them regularly as well. You want to make sure that your list is an "opt-in" list. This means that people have asked for you to put them on your list. They have OPTED to be on the list.

The most responsive list will always be your own IN-HOUSE list. These are names you have generated from attendees at your seminars or those who have come in through your Web site. Those people who come to one of your events or have opted in on your Web site will be highly likely to attend future events. If you've done a great job.

The funnels system starts by getting people who are potential buyers of your products and services to identify themselves. Once they identify themselves to you and give you their contact information, they are in your FUNNEL. You should then start mailing them a series of offers to get them to buy your initial low priced product.

The goal is to fill your funnel as quickly and as inexpensively as possible with people who are interested in the products and services you have to offer.

The lowest price products in your funnel may be under $10 reports. The next step up the price ladder might be a physical or an ebook at $27 or $37. More expensive items might include a newsletter subscription ($97) and an audio tape course ($197). A one day seminar might be priced at $297.

These prices are just examples. You may end up pricing them very differently in your own target market. The point is that you need to get people into your funnel. Once you capture their contact information (in your database) you want to get them to buy something from you.

Once they buy something from you, you want to trade them up to buy more and more products and services that you offer.

Your database is the backbone of your funnel system.

If you're speaking at someone else's event or giving a presentation to an association or corporation, make sure to get the list of attendees.

I like to mail to the list immediately after the event. Send it quickly, while your name is still fresh in their minds.

Keep people on your database until they ask you to be removed. I used to hear people say: "keep them on until they buy or die." I agree, but add . . . or until they ask to be removed. Never keep people on a list who don't want to be on it. It's a complete waste of your time.

The Single Most Important Formula in the Seminar Business

The most important formula in the seminar business is:
TR = SR + PS + CB

Total Revenue equals Seminar Registration + Product Sales + Consulting Business

Two of these items can easily be tallied immediately after your event. The dollars that come in from consulting work that you generate may go on for years after you do a seminar. Nice!

Seminar registration is the total number of dollars you generate from people who attend your event.

Product sales are orders that come in at your event and at any point after the seminar from those who attended your event to begin with.

Consulting business comes in over a much longer period of time. It is also the item that can be your biggest revenue item. Not long ago someone attended a $297 seminar of mine. They then bought the $777 package at the seminar. They then called up two months later and asked how much it would be to consult with me for 3 hours every month.

Understanding this formula is the difference between profit and loss in many cases. The uninformed observer will often conclude that you're not making any money when they show up at the hotel where you are giving seminars and count the number of people who come through your doors.

They are not computing the two additional factors that are so crucial to your long term success. The sale of products and the future consulting business that results. Registration dollars come in immediately. Product sales come in immediately for the most part. True, if you market correctly, orders for products should come in for the foreseeable future. Consulting business might come in forever.

*D*eveloping Your Career in Seminars

A career in seminars can be lucrative, enjoyable, helpful to others, and generally satisfying. But, like all careers and professions, public speaking and seminar presentation require that you **develop** your skills. Just starting with something you do well, building a seminar or workshop around it, and then resting on your laurels may work for a short period of time. But eventually you get knocked off your perch by someone willing to spend the time and money and energy to keep growing.

In this chapter, we'll look at some of the on-going steps you should take to keep your skills as a seminar-giver and your knowledge of your subject area current and ahead of the competition.

Study Other Speakers

If you're going to be in the seminar/speaking business you have to watch others who are in the field. In fact, don't just watch them, study them!

Write down what you see and hear that you like and things you don't like. Don't try to copy other speakers and seminar leaders, but do try to incorporate the things you like into your events.

Watch Good Movies, Read Good Books

Closely observing how good movies and books are constructed will help you in designing your seminars. Think about the way a good book or movie sucks you in immediately and how it keeps you intrigued and interested. This should be your goal at your event.

Watching good movies and reading good books has another advantage besides giving you a feel for how your seminar should "flow." If

---

you're reading and watching what your attendees are reading and watching, you'll be able to use current stories to which your audience can relate.

Enhance Your Image as an Expert

Establishing yourself as an expert will make it easier to get people to attend your events. The more visible you are in your marketplace (everything else being equal), the better the chances you'll have of getting people to register for your events and to tell others about them.

Here are some specific things I recommend you do to establish yourself as an expert. You may or may not be able to do all of them, but you should do as many as you can.

Writing a book

If you have written a book on a topic, you're the *de facto* expert in the field. A book can help you in so many ways. I consider it the most important single thing you can do to establish expertise and help build your business.

You may see clearly that you *need* a book but feel uneasy about trying to write one. You may think you don't have time or that your writing isn't good enough. You can solve these problems in a number of ways. Contact our sister company, Publishing Profit, Inc. (www.publishingprofit.com) for help finding a ghost writer or an editor or even a writing coach.

If you want more information about how to put a book together, pick up a copy of one of my other books, *Publishing for Maximum Profit*.

Generating publicity for yourself

The more often you appear in the media, the more people will look at you as the expert on your chosen topic. Look for ways to generate press for yourself. The resource section of this book suggests a number of ways you can go about increasing your publicity.

Posting messages in user groups

There is at least one Web-based news group for every industry. You should be a member of these news groups in any case because it's a great place to listen in on what your customers and prospects are thinking about. You can post your thoughts and ideas on these user groups and become a part of the conversational flow. Pithy remarks with substance in your field of expertise will get you noticed.

Be careful here, though. Anything that even faintly resembles advertising or self-promotion may well be viewed by other members of the group as impolite. You can spend a lot of time undoing the personal damage for being imprudent on a user group discussion board. This is a place for you to provide information. Promotion will naturally follow and usually take place in private email exchanges with interested members of the group who find your insights useful.

Scouting trade shows

Just as it is important to attend seminars and workshops where your target audience is learning about your topic, so it is vital that you attend the major trade shows in your field. You can learn a lot at a trade show. You can also make valuable contacts among people who are possible suppliers of information or products and services as well as prospective attendees. You can scout out potential outside speakers. You can collect all kinds of free literature and even samples you can use later to augment your present understanding of what's going on in your area of interest.

Trade shows are generally a very sound investment of time and money.

Attending other peoples' seminars

If you're going to be in this industry, you'll have to attend a lot of other peoples' seminars to build your knowledge base.

For example, some of my major markets are authors, speakers and consultants. I try to attend the major trade shows and seminars in each of these fields. You have to be selective or you'll be spending all your time and money attending these events. Be selective, but go.

Attend seminars where you'll both learn a lot and find good prospects for your products and services. The key at these events is to ask great questions strategically and contribute "brilliant" comments early in the event. Look for your opportunities and pounce on them. People will come up to you at the breaks and ask for your card and contact information.

Networking with the movers and shakers

Find people who are the "in crowd" in your market and get to know them. Befriend them. Find ways to help them and they will in turn help you.

Try this easy technique with people with whom you wish to ingratiate yourself. Go up and introduce yourself and ask "How can I help you?" By pre-empting the conversation and making yourself the one offering assistance, you make yourself a very popular person indeed!

Keep Files of Stories, Quotations and Statistics

You need to keep files of three major types of items: stories, quotations and statistics. Separate them by topics or subject matter so you can find appropriate ones to use later on.

Don't worry about where you'll use these bits of information. Just get them into your computer. You'll find places to use the good ones.

By the way, you don't need to go buy some big, expensive relational database program to store this stuff. My partner and colleague Dan Shafer, who is a real technology guru besides being a renowned writer and speaker, recommends a simple shareware program called EZGather for the storage of information like notes, quotations, and statistics. You can get a 30-day free trial of the program at www.unvisibleuniverse.com/infoEZgather.html and the shareware registration fee is only $10. The program works on Macs and on Windows machines and is ridiculously easy to use.

Cultivate Characteristics of a Great Speaker

Over the three or so years I presented CareerTrack seminars, I did a survey on the sly. I would ask participants at these events to write down what they thought were the three most important characteristics of a great speaker.

I did not give them any other coaching. I just asked that question and repeated it exactly the same way if they didn't quite hear it right. Over the course of a year I did this informal survey many times and got a total of about 2500 responses to this question.

They would write down their answers on a slip of paper and hand them to me at the end of the seminar.

I compiled the results and this is how they came out. Although there were other answers, these three were at the top and ranked in this order. All other answers accounted for less than 20% of the total answers.

This survey demonstrated that great speakers must be seen as sincere, knowledgeable, and humorous.

Sincere

The top item on the list was sincerity. People want a speaker they feel is "real." Nothing turns people off more quickly than someone pretending to be someone they aren't.

Everyone knows this intuitively. The question is how we create sincerity. What are the behavioral manifestations of sincerity? When people say, "That speaker really meant what he/she was saying," what caused them to say that? I have found four elements to be the greatest contributors to what we all know and perceive as sincerity.

First, you must **speak in a conversational tone**. A tone that people will feel is how you normally talk as a person in your everyday life.

This is one of the reasons I think that Oprah is so successful. When you listen to her, you get the feeling she is really the person you hear and see on TV.

One of my favorite professional speakers, Lou Heckler, personifies this sincerity. If you don't know who he is, you should. Call the National Speakers Association (contact information is in Appendix A) and get one of his tapes.

Another necessary ingredient to convey sincerity is to speak only about things you really believe in, and **feel passionate** about. Speakers who claim to "talk about anything" will fall flat on their faces in this area. There is no way anyone can truly feel passionate about everything (or maybe anything) they speak about.

Third, to be sincere in your presentation, you need a high degree of comfort about your **in-depth knowledge** of the material. Whatever your topic, you need to be an eager and interested student.

I have always had a passion for marketing. I read every book, attend every seminar, and buy every tape on the subject. Over the past 10 years, I have spent more than $100,000 in my study of marketing. When I speak on this topic, one of the things that contributes to my being perceived as sincere is my knowledge about the topic. (My passion also comes through loudly and clearly.)

Pick a topic area that you really enjoy and really study it. Read everything you can find about it. Know the field inside and out. Keep current with the latest trends and ideas. If you try to do all of this with a topic and find it to be drudgery, you haven't chosen the right topic.

Someone talked to me not long ago about what they were going to do when they retire. I don't understand retirement. If you love what you do, shouldn't you want to do it forever? My Dad is now 87. He has written 17 books and he didn't start until he was 65! He couldn't have done that unless he loved to write. If I live to the same age, I am sure I will still be a serious student of marketing.

Finally, let people know something about who you are as a person. Let them know some of your secrets. Don't tell them things that aren't relevant to the topic, but feel free to let them in on things that would help them. People will connect with you as a real person if you do this. They, in turn, will be more likely to be open with you and that two-way communication can lead to lots of great benefits.

One way to get your audience to identify with you is to let them know of places where you stumbled before you learned a lesson you are about to offer or have just explained. Let them see your humanity.

Knowledgeable

The second characteristic that makes a great speaker, according to the audiences I surveyed, was content. People do not want to listen to a speaker who doesn't deliver solid, useable information. How does one insure that this happens? Here are a few simple steps.

First, you must deliver information that is practical and easily applied. You should make it crystal clear how people can use this information. Give them all the tools. Nothing should be left to chance. At the end of your seminar or speech, people should not be left thinking: "OK, what do I do now?"

Second, you must clearly lay out the steps to follow to implement your practical advice. The best way to do this is in a handout that details everything they need to do. If you have ever bought a product that needs assembly, just think about how you have felt when the directions they included were poor. If you give poor directions to your audience on the how-to side, they will judge you as weak in the area of content.

Third, hang each of your major points on a hook that will enable your attendees to recall them quickly after they've left the seminar. In addition to your handout, you need to tell a story, or give an example that people will remember. Attendees need an "anchor" to store the concept. Stories and examples are the best and most memorable hooks. It is common for people to remember the stories long after they've forgotten the point. Of course, remembering the story leads to remembering the point!

Fourth, use a variety of teaching methods during the seminar. Everyone learns differently. Make sure you understand this when you are trying to give your great content retention value. Some people will need to see something, perhaps some kind of a prop or visual aid. Others will need to hear something to remember it. The story idea works well for these people. Still others will need to apply the concept to remember the content point. Create an exercise where they have to **do** something.

Mix all of these techniques throughout your seminar. Ideally, you provide something for each of these audiences for each major point in your presentation.

Humorous

In my survey, the third most important characteristic of a good speaker was humor.

There are three key things you should do to make your speech or seminar more humorous.

The best humor is self-deprecating. Make yourself the butt of all the jokes you use. This will endear you to the audience. It shows you have a lot of confidence in yourself. Otherwise, you wouldn't be very likely to show people that you screw up. Another big advantage to self-deprecating humor is that you avoid the risk of offending someone in the audience by picking on some group or personality type.

Remember, only a Catholic can tell a joke that seems to make Catholics look foolish. Anyone else will appear to be insensitive and bigoted. (In fact, in our increasingly politically sensitive culture, even a Catholic might not get away with a Catholic joke any more. Just don't risk it.)

Tell stories, not jokes. If you tell a joke and it doesn't work, everyone knows it. No one laughs. And with a joke, there is no getting around the fact that it didn't work. When you set up a joke, everyone knows what that setup looks like. They also know what people thought of the joke by the amount of laughter you get.

When you tell what you think to be a funny story and no one laughs, everyone will just think it was a story. Because a story lacks the joke set-up, there's no built-in expectation that the story will be funny. If it is funny, people will laugh. If it isn't, it will just seem like another story. Less harm done.

This leads to the last point I'll make on humor. **It's only funny if they laugh**. The definition of funny must come from the people receiving the message. I don't care if you think a joke is funny. I don't care if your family thinks it is funny. It is **not** funny if people don't laugh.

If you tell a story to be funny and it doesn't get a laugh, you need to drop that story in future seminars and speeches. Your audience is the only true judge of humor.

By the way, I've seen a lot of people try to take this advice only to mess it up by introducing the story with something like this: "I have a funny story that will illustrate what I mean." Don't do that. As I said, your audience will tell you if it's funny. If you have to tell them in advance, it's a good sign it isn't.

Many professional comedians start with a collection of jokes. When they deliver them, people might laugh at five of them. They keep those five and add a bunch of new ones. People might laugh at six of the new ones, so the comedian will then keep those six that work. The comedian now has 11 jokes that work. Then they repeat the process.

I'm not saying you should become a comedian on stage. But I am saying that my survey indicates that if you want to be considered a great speaker, you have to be perceived as funny. This doesn't mean that every story you tell has to be funny, but if you follow the steps above, at least more of them will. This in turn enhances your chances of being perceived as a great speaker, which helps you sell more products. And that, after all, is the point of all of this!

Keep Improving Yourself Professionally

Last year I spent over $17,000 on books, tapes, and educational seminars. Why? Because I have to keep current in my field. Since I'm also passionate about my field (back to sincerity), this isn't a burden but a joy.

If you're not interested in delivering the best seminar you possibly can, you probably don't need to be reading this book. Don't get me wrong. I'm not some Goody Two-Shoes who feels you should want to be and do your best work because it's the "right" thing to do (although it is). You should do your best because it's in your financial interest to do so. People will come back to other events you do and the word about how good you are will spread.

To do the best seminar possible, you need to educate yourself. In one of my niche markets I have a competitor who presents a lot of seminars. I sat in on one of their seminars a few years back. When I went back a few years later and sat in on a portion of the same seminar, I found that they hadn't changed a word. That is ridiculous.

If you need to spend money to learn as much as you can about your topic, do it. Read books. Read newsletters. Read trade publications. Attend seminars in your field. Attend seminars in related fields. Get on-line regularly and search for the key words in your field. Go as deeply into your topic as you can.

As a seminar leader, you need to study on another front as well. You also need to get as much education as you can in the areas of how to improve your seminar marketing and delivery.

You owe it to yourself, and you owe it to your audience.

Develop and Exploit Your Own Style

Your personal style when you do your seminar is critical to your success. You need to develop a speaking and presentation style that identifies you as the person you want to be.

Most important is that you don't violate the rule of being yourself. Your style is composed of a number of different elements. These include, but are not limited to: the way you deliver information, the way you dress, and the way you respond to people.

My speaking style is very direct and somewhat confrontational. My style will sometimes get people angry. Be careful not to be overly confrontational; people have to like you to want to buy additional products or services from you.

I have learned one universal law as it relates to style over the years — people must LIKE you. If they don't like you they won't listen to you. If they don't listen to you, they won't buy from you. But remember, no one can be universally liked. Hey, some people hated Ghandi!

I have a trademark style of dress. I'm never the one with a suit. I'm the one dressed in dress slacks with **very** colorful "Coogi" sweaters, the only name-brand product I've ever worn in my life. I love them. They happen to be very expensive. Since I'm known as an extremely frugal guy, this may seem somewhat inconsistent.

I bought my first Coogi sweater in Australia for less than half of what I'd have had to pay in the United States. I still own only three of them. I rotate them so it doesn't look like I'm always wearing the same one. But this has become part of my style.

Another element of style is how accessible you choose to be. Some speakers like to remain extremely accessible during breaks, before and after seminars, and even via email. Others like to cultivate the feeling of the aloof expert with whom you must make an appointment. There is a case to be made for doing both. I like to play the accessible expert because, frankly, I like people. Many well-known consultants do not, or at least appear by their behavior not to do so. Frankly, I feel badly for them.

Again, don't violate the rule of being yourself. Don't try to be gregarious if you're not. Create your personal style from the cards you've been dealt.

As a result of the style that you select to use (either consciously or unconsciously) some people won't like you. This is inevitable. People tend either to hate me or love me. I actually prefer it that way myself. The more direct and "in-your-face" your style, the more apt this is to happen.

After you select your style, don't try to change it unless you have good reason. If **most** people like you, you're probably in good shape. There will always be a certain number of people who just can't stand you. You know what? That's life. Live with it!

My seminar delivery is very fast and rapid fire. I do this because it's my style. I also do it because I find that if you go just a little faster than people can understand, you'll end up selling a lot more product. Follow my lead on this one. Move quickly because of all the great material you have to share with them.

Take Care of Your Voice

If the majority of your revenue comes from doing seminars, your voice is your most important "tool." Many people do things that cause their instrument harm.

I had a colleague at CareerTrack named Roger Burgraff. Roger is a speech expert. He knows a lot about the physical mechanics of the voice. Roger always made some very important points about the "care and feeding" of a speaker's voice.

Here are some of the highlights about what he had to say:

First, never yell. It is incredibly damaging to your vocal chords. If you're tempted to go to a sporting event where you know you'll get riled up, stay home!

Second, when you're not speaking, keep your mouth shut. Don't sing in the car or talk on the phone. Give your vocal chords a chance to rest.

Third, drink room-temperature (decidedly **not** ice-cold) water while you speak. Just like a car needs oil, your voice needs water to be properly lubricated. I always squeeze a lemon or two into a large carafe of water. As far as I know, the lemon itself did no harm or good, it just made it easier for me to suck down all the water. At a one-day seminar I might go through a gallon of water. (Yes, that leads to lots of breaks designed to let me run to the bathroom. But your audience likes breaks; we'll talk about that later.)

Fourth, never drink anything containing caffeine. It's bad for your throat and voice.

Fifth, watch out for dairy products. They tend to create mucus, not a good thing to be "hacking up" in front of your audience. Some people can get away with it. Check to see how milk and other products react with your own voice.

Ease Your Way in: Continuing Education Classes

Most cities have places where you can teach classes. Many of these venues are non-traditional continuing education centers. They are great places to get practice and you'll make a little money. They also allow you to test concepts and ideas with very little risk.

Before you start, you should make sure that they allow you to sell your products. I never ask. I just do it. In most cases they are paying you so little they won't object. As long as you follow my rules on **how** to sell your product, your sales efforts probably won't draw complaints from your attendees and the issue will just never come up.

Continuing education classes are where many people get started doing their speaking. In fact, I continue to do my workshops at these locations.

If you want to work with these folks, here is how to do it.

First, get the name of the "program director" or the person who makes the decisions and selects instructors.

Second, you need to send a letter.

In that letter, follow this progression.

In the first paragraph, personalize the letter to the individual. Say that you are submitting the following materials to see if they can be included in their course catalog.

In the second paragraph in bold type put the course title, subtitle, and a one-sentence description of the class.

In the third paragraph, describe how attendees will benefit.

In the fourth paragraph, present the rationale for why you are uniquely qualified to present this class. Describe your experience, credentials, materials you publish on the topic (like a newsletter, a set of tapes, a public seminar, and your all-important book).

On the second page, create a course description. Basically, design the ad they could put into their catalog. Make it short and snappy. Give it a compelling title and a great description. Keep the description to a maximum of 200 words. Use bullet points for the hot stuff.

On the third page, put your complete resumé or biography. Include everything you can to make you look like **the** guru on the topic. This will be different for each class. For whatever class you propose, skew your resumé in that direction.

In an appendix put everything you have to back up all of your claims. Letters of recommendation, press releases, possibly even a set of materials (books and tapes). If you have a video of you doing a presentation, include that as well.

Follow up a few days after you send your letter. Don't become a pest, but persistence pays here as in so many other promotional and marketing situations.

Finally, contact all the continuing education venues in your area, not just one!

Dealing With Unpaid Speaking Invitations

As your notoriety as a speaker grows, you will almost certainly be invited to speak for no fee at other peoples' seminars, at conferences, and similar places. I have one basic rule about such invitations. I accept them only if they allow me to sell my products from the podium during the event.

Unless you're allowed to sell products, don't do the gig. With your own events, you control the show so this isn't a problem. The only exception to this rule would be an organization where you feel the exposure would be so beneficial that it would be stupid to turn it down.

In my own case I can only think of three places where I would go for a no-fee, no product sales arrangement. One would be with the Million Dollar Round Table (MDRT). The second is with The Young Presidents Organization (YPO). And the final one is as a faculty member of the Income Builders International Free Enterprise Forum.

Know What You MUST Know About the Competition

As with every business, you'll have competition. If you don't have any, you should be worried. This would mean that there may not be any demand for the kind or type of event you're thinking of promoting. Since you have some competition, it's a good idea to learn all you can about them.

Start your search on-line. If you're doing a marketing seminar for chiropractors, go to your favorite search engines and enter in the words: "marketing seminar for chiropractors." You'll also want to search for variations on these terms as well. Look everywhere you can on-line and you'll find what you're looking for. (If you want help with this, buy my friend and colleague Dan Shafer's amazing eBook, *How to Find Anything on the Web in Less Than 10 Minutes*, which is being published at the same time as this book. It's available through our joint Web site, www.publishingprofit.com.)

You'll also want to approach trade associations. Act like a naïve "newbie" and tell them you're looking for a certain kind of event and ask who offers them.

As soon as you decide to do seminars in a given topic or area, attend every seminar that anyone else offers that is remotely related. Take extensive notes at these events. Monitor them not just for the information, but for how they present the content. Take what you can from their events and make changes where you feel they're appropriate.

Talk to attendees. Ask them what they liked the most and least about the event. You can learn a lot by surveying the people who are there. Remember, their perspective will be very different from yours. They will be your future customers. While you're at it, collect business cards for your database. They will be ideal prospects for your events.

Make sure that you are on the mailing lists for all of your competitors. Do this both on and offline. If they take you off their lists because they identify you, just ask a friend to get on their list and send you their promotions. (When competitors find their way onto my mailing lists, I don't try and make it difficult for them. It actually takes too much work to ferret out a competitor.)

After attending their events, assess where their strengths and weaknesses lie. Assess your own skill and knowledge base and see where you can provide a different approach or where you can fill in the gaps and do some coaching work.

An example from the publishing industry may help to illustrate my point. I help small to medium sized publishers make more money. There are two or three people who do something related. When I started this business, I attended their events.

My assessment turned up that although the individuals sponsoring these events were intelligent and knowledgeable, their content and presentation were lacking. I came in and quickly gained huge market share at their expense by providing a much better seminar with a slightly different slant.

As soon as you identify your competition, you'll want to see if they are amenable to a joint venture. In this case, a "joint venture" is a relationship in which they let you mail a promotion about your event to their customer base and you cut them in for 50% of what you make from their customers who attend. In many cases, you'll be met by immediate hostility. Very few people can see the positive benefits to them of a joint venture for your seminar. They may or may not be right.

Here's how I see it. If I'm **really** good at what I do, I won't be scared to let my customers know about a seminar from one of my competitors. Why? Because they will inevitably be disappointed. I might as well get paid 50% by them to let them know about an event they will probably find on their own.

Another thing to remember about people and seminars. Many people will hop from guru to guru looking for the next greatest idea in a field. Still others just want to listen to everyone's perspective on a given topic. Understanding these realities, it behooves you to make some money from your database in exchange for introducing them to the other gurus in the field. After all, they are highly likely to find them anyway. If they find them on their own, you won't make a dime!

*D*esigning and Creating the Seminar

Setting Measurable Goals for Your Event

I have three goals when I give a seminar. First, I want to get great evaluations. Second, I want to sell a lot of product. Third, I want to achieve both of these goals in such a way that people will enthusiastically want to do business with me again.

All three of these can be measured. This is essential. I don't want any of my goals to be subjective and therefore nebulous. How can you tell whether or not you are achieving goals that aren't well defined? You can't. It's that simple.

I suggest you ask yourself the same questions with regards to the seminars you conduct. How will you determine if your seminars are successful? Make sure all the items are measurable.

The numbers on your evaluations will tell you whether or not people like and respect you. If you're asking people to rate you on a five-point scale, set an average evaluation threshold. That might be 3 or 3.5 or 4, for example, depending on your expectations of yourself.

Product sales are discussed in detail in another section of this book, but you need a consistent, cross-seminar way of judging the return on investment you make in your seminars. I use a yardstick of revenue per person per minute. If you have 100 people in the room and sell $10,000 and you do it in a 50 minute speech you'd be doing $2 per person, per minute. Is that good? That depends on your goal and your previous experience. For me, $2/person/minute is good, $3/person/minute would be great, anything over that amount would be phenomenal.

Use the same yardstick to measure every event so you can compare your results over time and across numerous events accurately.

The only way to measure repeat business and referrals is carefully tracking the number of repeat and referral customers that come through your doors. This requires some advance planning. There has to be some way for you to know when you receive an order that it's from someone who has attended one of your events. There also has to be some system of referrals so that when a new order comes in as a result of a referral, you can know and track that.

Selecting Your Topic

I conduct a lot of seminars on the topic of giving seminars. At these events people sometimes get up in front of the group and tell us they can do a seminar on any topic. That is simply absurd.

If you can talk about **any** topic, then you clearly aren't an **expert** on any topic. Your audience wants to hear experts when they go to a seminar. Or at least people they perceive to be experts.

To decide on a topic you have to ask yourself two questions. First, what do you have a background in? Second, what do you have a passion for?

At least for your first seminar product, start with what you already know.

Don't be discouraged if others are already doing seminars in the area you're interested in. All this tells you is that there is demand for the topic. I would be much more concerned for you if you told me that no one was doing a seminar on your topic. This could mean that there is no demand for seminars on that particular topic.

Assuming you find some competition, check it out (see Chapter 3) and then figure out where the gaps are, either in knowledge and expertise or in quality of seminar presentation. Then, when you put your seminar together, fill in as many of those gaps as you can. At the very least, put your peculiar slant on the information and make it your own.

It's no secret that Tony Robbins took an existing technology (neuro-linguistic programming, or NLP) and put his own (very commercial) slant on the concepts. This was brilliant on his part. It also proves that the first person in the market isn't always the person that does it best or makes the most money.

Titling Your Event

There are two ways to go when you create the title to your event. If you or your firm is a well-known entity or celebrity in your field, put your name or your firm's name front and center in the title.

If you're Michael Jordan and you're doing a basketball seminar, you have to put your name in the title. It might be: "Michael Jordan Talks Basketball." The primary reason why people will show up for an event has to do with Michael Jordan himself. In an example like this, Michael Jordan could be talking about basket-weaving and people would still show up. They are showing up to see him.

I've got minor celebrity status in a number of my niche markets. I encourage you to strive to achieve some fame in your niche, too. But before you get to that point, you'll have to use another method of titling your events to maximize registration.

I suggest you use the following formula for creating your titles. Take your biggest benefit and match it with your attendees' greatest needs. In one of my markets I do a seminar on marketing. I title it: "How to Competition-Proof Your Video Production Business."

This title combines my greatest benefit (marketing information) with my attendees' greatest need (dealing with competition). I've also used a title like: "51 Marketing Secrets of Self-Storage Marketing Success." This is effective because of its specificity. People want to know what all 51 of them are.

Another familiar way to do things is to do the: "How to blank, so that you can blank." This is a very familiar formula that can also be effective. How do you know which one will work best? You don't. You have to test alternatives to see what works.

If you're thinking of a title, shoot me an email (fgleeck@aol.com) and I'll give you my feedback. But don't send it to me if you don't want an honest appraisal!

Structuring and Designing Your Seminar

How do you create the seminar content? How do you decide what to include and what to leave out? How do you figure out the best sequence in which to present your material? Many seminar neophytes get so hung up on this point that they never get their seminars created! But I've developed a simple system to help you over this hurdle. Follow it and you won't encounter any obstacles to structuring and designing your seminar.

My Basic System

First, brainstorm all the topics that you think need to be covered at the event. Don't stop during this process to critique what you're writing. Just get them all written down.

After you've exhausted every single little, eensy, meansy idea you want to cover, go back and group the ideas together into logically connected "clumps". This sounds harder than it really is; once you've done this the first time, you'll see how your subject-matter expertise pays off. Now, decide which ideas should be major topics and which should be supporting points or issues under each of the "main" topics.

Shoot for a minimum of 25 **major** topics. Then try to have a minimum of four subpoints under each of these main points.

Some people like to put all of these ideas on index cards and lay them on the ground or a big table. Then they go back and sort them into piles and determine which piles should go first and what the heading or title should be for each pile. Whatever works for you — **just do it**! I use a computer for this task most of the time, but I still occasionally use the index card technique.

Using this system will help you to create your seminar outline almost instantly. After you get this first step done, then you have to decide what order everything should go in.

There are some basic sequences that recur in nature and in most fields of knowledge. It is likely, though not mandatory, that you will find one of these works for your topic.

You might find that a basics-to-advanced approach works best for your material. Begin with the information your audience has to understand before it can take advantage of the deeper knowledge later in the seminar. (But be careful; if your seminar is aimed at people who have some experience in the field, what is "basic" might be overly simple to them. Gauge your audience's starting point and make **that** your "basic" level.)

Another approach that works well in many situations is general-to-specific. You begin with the broad coverage of the topic that puts everyone on the same page, then drill down into details as you get more and more specific or focused throughout the seminar.

Finally, some topics lend themselves to a very clear sequential order. First, you have to do this. Then you take this step. If that's the case, your outline is done for you (always assuming, of course, that you know the topic well.)

After you put it in the order you think would work, put your work aside for a day or two. When you go back, see if the order still makes sense. If it does, keep it that way. If not, make changes. You might also want to run it by a colleague or two to see if anything obvious is missing or misplaced.

Finally, come up with a great introduction and a great conclusion (we'll talk about these more specifically shortly). Remember the primacy-recency effect. We remember most what we hear first and last.

After putting everything in order, ask yourself some additional questions.

Exercise: Is there an exercise that would be appropriate to illustrate this point or issue?

Quotation: Do I have a quotation that would fit to better illuminate this point?

Statistic: Can I locate a statistic that would help make this module more clear?

Visual Aid: Would a visual aid be appropriate to use with this module, or am I just using it for its own sake?

Story: Do I have a story that would be appropriate to make this module come alive?

Prop: Can a prop be used to better illustrate?

Example: Can you come up with an example that would help to illustrate this point?

Book/Other reference: Can you head people to a reference source if they want more information about this?

As you remember or uncover such supplemental materials, add them to your presentation notes.

After you've done this, you're ready to present the seminar.

If you're like me (and I know I am!) you don't need to script your presentation word for word. I just like to work from an outline. I suggest you do the same. It will be more natural, interruptions will be less disruptive and problematic, and you'll seem like more of an expert to your audience.

Using My Modular Content-Creation System

When I create content for my seminars or bootcamps, I always create things in modules. A module is a nugget of information roughly corresponding to one of the 25 main topics we just discussed. A module can represent a few minutes to as much as a half-hour of presentation time, though most will be five to 15 minutes long.

After you've created your modules, you can put them in your "virtual jukebox." Let's assume you have put together 500 modules. When you do another event you can go to your virtual jukebox and use module numbers 33, 48, 159, etc. After you put all of those in place you might only have to develop 8 or 10 other modules to create a whole new seminar.

As you do more presentations, you'll accumulate more and more modules. Your jukebox will have more and more "songs" that you can play. Naturally, you'll have to update your modules on occasion, but you'll have much less work than starting from scratch.

Use this system and content creation will become a breeze!

Creating a Dynamite Opening and Closing

Psychology calls it the "primacy-recency" effect. People tend to remember what they hear first and what they hear last more effectively than all of the stuff that comes between. This being the case, you need to create a dynamite opening and closing to your presentation. If your event consists of more than one presentation, it will also pay to take time to formulate a great opening and closing to the event.

The only way to do this is through trial and error. The best way to conduct this experimentation is to speak at venues where you can test your openings and closings to see what works. Also, you'll need different opening-closing combinations for different events. A great opening for one program may be inappropriate for another event. The same thing goes for your closings.

Fabulous Openings

Your opening has three primary goals.

First, it needs to get peoples' attention.

Second, it needs to set up your audience for the information you'll be delivering. That means it must be relevant. You can't tell that story about growing up in Alaska as the son of a fisherman if it doesn't tie into your subject matter.

Finally, your opening should position you as a top expert in the field. Make sure to weave information into your opening to make this clear to your audience.

Do **not** open a seminar by going through all of the administrative and housekeeping details. You can always go back after a few minutes and tell people where the bathrooms are. Get them off on the right foot with some great, high-quality information.

Powerful Closings

A great closing will help you increase product sales and consulting business. You should test various approaches to your closing, zeroing in on one that works best for your audience and their needs.

Your closing should have two primary goals.

First, it must reinforce the notion that you are **the** expert in your field.

Second, it should highlight the key things you want your audience to remember about the material you've presented.

Before my official close, I almost always include two exercises I suggest you consider using.

First, I like people to pull out their action idea sheets (an idea discussed earlier). If you've caught on to the power of using these sheets, you will have been reviewing them after each break.

At the beginning of the event, I promise attendees that they will leave with at least a certain number of action ideas. Before I close, I always ask the group how many people got at least as many action ideas as I promised. If I've done things right, they've gotten at least twice that many.

When everyone has their hands raised I ask a few select people from the audience exactly how many they've gotten. The number is usually a minimum of twice what I promised.

The second exercise I conduct just before closing is to go around the room and ask people to name the first 3 things they will do when they get back to their home or office. If the group is small enough, I let everyone chime in. If not, I ask a few people around the room.

With that reinforcement in mind, I go to my powerful close that summarizes the key points I've shared and reconfirms my role as the subject-matter expert.

Preparing Handouts and Workbooks

The proper design of your handouts and workbooks at your events is extremely important. People who go to events longer than an hour or two in length expect to receive a handout or workbook.

I have seen more than one marketing "guru" give a high-priced seminar and not provide a single handout. Nothing! This makes no sense to me. I had to conclude one of two things about this individual. Either he was lazy or he had some secret motive for doing things this way. I have not yet been able to convince myself that any valid motive exists for this kind of oversight.

For any event of two hours or less, put together a handout. If it's a short presentation, put together a short handout. It should be no more than three pages. For an event from half a day to a full day, you need to put together a small workbook of 20-40 pages. The shorter the event, the lower the number of pages.

Events that are longer than a day should be enlarged accordingly. I've seen five-day events where attendees receive huge three-ring binders. If your event is highly experiential, you may be able to get away with giving away less paper.

The outline you created for the seminar becomes the skeleton for your workbook. Take your outline and include some of the sub-points under each major topic. I recommend you make your handout or workbook somewhat interactive. Have participants fill in the blanks and do other clever things to get them to interact with the workbook. But, don't overdo it.

You'll also want to include other supporting documents: articles you've written, articles others have written, lists of resources, and anything else you think would be helpful to support your material.

You must also include a table of contents for your event. Let people know what is going to be covered and in what order. (Remember, however, not to include specific time frames for each topic, just in case you have to change the times.)

Include your bio, customized to this specific seminar. Highlight points that are relevant to your attendees.

Include as many samples as you can. Do this within the bounds of cost constraints. Unfortunately, the larger your handout or workbook, the more it will cost you. A binder that runs 200 pages will cost you upwards of $10 per attendee. Give them as much as they need, but don't break the bank.

Particularly if you're taping the event but even if you're not, you should include in the handout hard copies of all of your visuals. Obviously, people who buy the tape(s) of the event won't be able to see the things you're pointing to on the screen in front of the audience, so including them in hard-copy form is essential.

At the back of every handout or workbook, I include a list of people and firms I recommend. Rather than just use the term "references," I like to call it my "Million-Dollar Rolodex." It sounds sexier and gives the perception of much greater value.

Something I have learned the hard way is that the workbook pages must be numbered. I like the idea of using letters to identify all the samples in the appendix. In the past I've tried to get people to look for things in the manual without numbered pages. I don't recommend it. You'll hear about it on the evaluations if you don't number the pages.

Never attach your order sheet to the handout you give to people at the beginning of a class. I just attended a workshop in which this was done. It will not help you to maximize sales and it annoys some people who perceive they are paying for your product pitch.

If you have guest speakers, get their handouts in advance. Make sure that if they have additional handouts outside your main handout, they have at least 10-20% more copies than you need. Insist that they give you a "clean" copy of the handout that they use at the time they speak. If you don't, you'll have to track them down later to get the handouts from them. When you have multiple speakers at a bootcamp, this can become a nightmare.

Also, if you intend to record and sell tapes of an event with multiple speakers, be careful! Tell each speaker not to make the handouts **too** long. All this will do is increase your cost of product and mailing when you duplicate and fulfill orders for the product you create.

Consider Offering a Bootcamp

Bootcamps are high-priced, multi-day seminars. In most cases there are numerous speakers.

You may also produce bootcamps where you don't speak at all but rather play the role of promoter and host. You could even try to do an entire bootcamp yourself. That would be very demanding, but it can be done.

Bootcamps are another high end product in the arsenal of products that you can offer people. People who attend your initial seminar or buy an inexpensive front-end product need to be offered high-end products. Bootcamps are definitely one of them.

Remember that people are most apt to buy the same kind of product they have bought in the past. People are also most likely to buy through the same channels they have bought from before.

This means that at the initial seminar you are highly likely to be able to sell people on attending another seminar. A high-priced bootcamp qualifies. Why? Because they have already self-selected. They are sitting there at the seminar. If they are impressed with you in a short form, they will probably "buy you" in the long form. The bootcamp.

One of the nicest things about bootcamps is that you usually don't have to travel. In most cases, you'll want to promote your bootcamps in your home city or locale. By careful design, I live in Las Vegas. It's easy to get people to come to me for events.

I am not saying that if you live in Bismarck, North Dakota, it will be impossible for you to get people to come to you, but you would be better advised to have everyone go to Aspen, instead.

Depending on your market and how your customers perceive you, you can often times get 3-5% of your in-house list to come to a bootcamp. Some people get an even higher response rate. It all depends on the market you're in, the degree of notoriety you have, the price of the event, and how well you've impressed your customers in the past.

Let's say you have 500 customers on your in-house list. This means that if you sent a bootcamp solicitation, you could expect to get somewhere between 15 and 25 people to show up and give you a lot of money for a three-day session where they come to sit at your feet. After all, you're the guru of whatever it is that you do.

We'll talk more in Chapter 7 about some of the techniques specific to marketing bootcamps that differ from those you'll use to market seminars and other, shorter events.

During a bootcamp, go longer than eight hours each day. This will make people feel like they are getting more than their money's worth.

I also like the idea of planning at least one "big event" for the group. If I'm doing a bootcamp in New York City it is usually a Broadway show. In Las Vegas it would be a show on the "Strip." I make it optional and people have to pay for it themselves. There is usually no resistance to the fact that they have to pay since they are already paying quite a bit to be there. Some people go, while others choose to do other things.

Planning the Event

Start With a Great Checklist

There are so many stupid little things you can't afford to forget in the seminar business that you must have a checklist of things to do and bring to any event.

I've given you a sample in Appendix A. There is only one way to develop one. First, brainstorm everything you think you'll need at an event. Then show that list to two or three other people. See if they can think of anything you may have forgotten.

Keep the list handy when you do your event. Write down anything that comes up while you're doing the seminar on the sheet itself. By the time you've done a few you'll have a pretty good list developed and you'll be less apt to forget anything crucial.

Make copies for each event and check the items off as you get them done.

Scheduling Considerations

I gave a seminar a number of years ago on Super Bowl Sunday. Bad idea! This is an extreme example but it illustrates an important point: give your seminar a greater chance of success by scheduling it on the right day(s) and in the right month. There's been a lot of research on this subject, so you don't need to guess.

Best Days to Schedule

There are a couple of basic principles to keep in mind when picking the day for a one-day event or the start-end days for a multi-day event.

Check the sporting events and national and religious holidays that might be held on a particular day. Even a major local festival or event can interfere with your conference's success. If you're not sure, ask! Contact the Chamber of Commerce in the city that you'll be working in. After doing that, check the internet. One site I like to use for this kind of thing is www.holidayfestival.com. That site lists all the holidays and festivals its operators can find and does a decent job of coverage.

Also make sure to check whether other industry events might be held on the same day. If you're on good terms with the trade organizations, you may not want to compete with them. In a couple of my niche markets I do exactly the opposite. I hold my events the day before they have industry trade shows. This is because they don't allow me to speak. So, the only way for me to get to this group is to compete with them.

I do events at the same time and in the same city as their major trade events. This way, people who want to hear me and attend my seminars don't have to make a special trip. All they have to do is add a few days to their schedule at an event they are already going to attend.

If a major industry event is happening in Chicago from Wednesday to Saturday the first week of May, I give my seminar on Tuesday in Chicago. As long as I mail out my promotion far enough in advance, this allows people to book their air travel so they can get in a day early for my event.

It's impossible to find the **perfect** day. Not long ago I arranged a bootcamp in the Las Vegas area on the same day that NASCAR was having one of their races. The problem wasn't that we were drawing from the same potential audience pool, the problem was that it ended up jacking up the hotel rates by double their normal amount. This was a problem!

The moral? Check to make sure that hotel space will be available. If you're doing an out of town seminar, you may want to check the Web sites of the local Chamber of Commerce and their major convention centers to make sure there isn't a conflict.

Research in the seminar field clearly shows that there are better and worse days to give seminars. The research, done years ago by Howard Shenson, still holds up today.

In this study, the numbers were compiled to see which days of the week pulled the greatest number of registrations.

The results varied somewhat based on whether or not the person attending was paying themselves or had an organization they worked for picking up the tab.

When Participant is Paying	When Someone Else is Paying
Saturday	Wednesday
Sunday	Thursday
Thursday	Tuesday
Wednesday	Friday
Tuesday	Saturday
Friday	Monday
Monday	Sunday

Best Months to Schedule

The same research that was done on days has been done to determine which months pull the best. Here are the results:

When Participant is Paying	When Someone Else is Paying
January	March
September	October
October	April
March	September
April	November
June	January
November	February
February	June
May	May
July	July
December	August
August	December

Does this mean that you shouldn't, under any circumstances, do a seminar in the months of July, August and December? No. But I would be **very** careful about doing them at that time.

Picking a Location

Your decision as to where to hold your seminars is an important one. The choice of where to hold your seminars will depend on a number of factors. I generally do my events in the major cities in the United States. This way those people who have to travel can get there easily.

Depending on your topic and what your goals are, you may want to do seminars in some of the smaller cities as well.

If you're just starting out, stick with Seattle, Portland, San Francisco, Los Angeles, Phoenix, Denver, Dallas, Houston, St. Louis, Kansas City, Chicago, Atlanta, Miami, Washington, New York, and Boston. This list might even be too big, depending on what you're doing, but it's a good place to start.

The more seminar cities you make available, the lower your attendance will be in each city (in most cases). Take a look at a publication that is updated yearly called Places Rated Almanac to help you figure out where you might want to do your seminars.

CareerTrack made their mark in the seminar business by going to the smaller, second- and third-tier cities. The idea was to bring the seminar to the people. If you consider doing the same, it will mean a lot of travel.

At this point, I mainly do seminars in either New York City or Las Vegas. I have residences in both, which makes it easy for me.

I will do events in other cities where I can piggyback on an industry event. All the people in the publishing world go to a thing called American Book Expo. I do seminars in the cities where they have their events and try to cannibalize their members and attendees.

One of my goals over the next few years is to be doing a lot more events in my "home" city. A big reason why I picked Las Vegas as my base of operations a few years back was because of the advantages it offered me for giving seminars. There are a lot of cheap, non-stop flights in and out of this city. In addition to that, hotel rooms are relatively inexpensive.

When people are deciding whether or not to come to your events, they factor in a number of elements. First, they consider the registration fee. Then they consider the cost of the airfare, hotel, rental car and expenses. After they add all of these elements up they assess whether or not it's worth it to attend.

Working with Hotels

You'll almost certainly want to host your event at a hotel. There are a lot of reasons for this, not the least of which is that they are a known quantity. Renting local meeting facilities can be risky unless you've done your homework and even at that they seldom have the supporting services you'll want: food, parking, copy center, phones, etcetera.

Stick with a well-known, name-brand, relatively classy chain. People will not want to spend $400 for your workshop and show up at a run-down Holiday Inn. The cost of meeting rooms at the better hotels isn't much more than at the poorer properties. You generally can't go wrong with a Marriott. They tend to have nice properties and great service.

One of the things that gets screwed up over 90% of the time is how they post the name of your event. Usually you'll have the event posted with the name of your company. I want to have them post the name of the seminar itself. Make sure you specify this when you talk with the hotel staff and confirm it the night before and the morning of the event.

Also, walk into the hotel as if you were an arriving attendee and ask them about the seminar. See if they can direct you to the right room. If they can't, make sure to give the staff an education about where you are and how to get to you. Alert everyone from the front desk people to the bell staff. Let everyone know who and where you are so no one has a problem finding you.

In Tampa there are at least two Marriotts. Be careful. This can pose big problems. Be sure to ask if there is any possible confusion that might occur. When people register, make sure they are aware of this fact. I had a problem in Tampa many years ago and learned from my mistake.

Hotels get away with murder. They charge ridiculous fees for food and beverage items. This is where they make their money. To avoid getting completely ripped off, remember these tips.

First, buy coffee by the gallon, not by the cup. You'll save a bundle. Also make sure that your coffee is inside your room. If it's in a common area you'll have everyone in the hotel drinking at your expense. If you catch other people drinking your refreshments, point it out immediately to the hotel staff. If they are good, they will adjust the bill to compensate for the problem.

If you're guaranteeing the hotel sleeping rooms (which we generally don't) you can usually get the room for free. The meeting rooms are not where hotels are looking to make their money. They want to get paid for sleeping rooms and the food and beverage business.

If you find a place in a city that you like, work with them repeatedly. They will get to know you and vice versa. It will make things a lot easier for everyone. If you're going to be doing a seminar in a certain city, call my office and find out if we have someone we use in that city. We'll be happy to share our contact with you.

If possible, visit the hotel in advance. This may not always be possible, but if it is, do so. This greatly reduces or eliminates the chances of big surprises when you show up.

What You MUST Know About Using Outside Speakers

When you promote a seminar or other event you have a choice. You can either do it entirely on your own or round up other speakers to participate.

If you do use outside speakers make sure you have seen them speak before asking them to participate. I've made the mistake twice of asking someone to speak at an event before I heard them. I'll never make the mistake again.

Also, make sure you give any and all of your speakers very specific instructions as to how you want them to deliver information and what their time frame will be. In the resource section of this book I've included a sample of what I give to speakers before they speak at my events.

Even when you do this you'll still have an occasional person that you wish you wouldn't have allowed a speaking slot.

Most of the time when you do a seminar or workshop, you are the sole speaker. You're the expert people come to hear. Besides, it's what you do.

But if you run a bootcamp or a multi-day event, or if you just want to engage in a bit of variety, you may find yourself tempted to use outside speakers. It's perfectly alright to do so, but you need to be aware of some possible pitfalls and of how to deal with those speakers professionally and credibly.

Pros and Cons of Using Outside Speakers

There are pluses and minuses to using outside speakers at your events. If you invite anyone else to speak at your events, you are taking a risk. If the person bombs, it's your fault. It doesn't matter why they flop, you will get the blame. There are, as you can guess, some pros and some cons to using outside speakers. Let's review the major issues on both sides of the coin.

Pros

Break up the monotony
People sometimes get bored just hearing one person talk continuously for an entire event. If you can find people who can add to your event, this alone **almost** makes it worth it to have them.

Additional expertise you don't have

You can't be an expert on everything. People don't expect you to be. You can deliver the best information possible to your audiences by using speakers who are knowledgeable in areas you don't know well.

Access their in-house lists

A big benefit to using other speakers is that you'll be able to mail to their in-house list. This should be a mandatory condition of their speaking at your event. Let's say that you're having a bootcamp and asking a dozen other speakers to contribute. If every speaker that you asked to speak had just 2,000 people in their email database you'd be able to mail to close to 25,000 people.

Since the response from one's in-house list is generally a lot higher than other promotions, you're in good shape. This will make it easy for you to pack the house for your event.

At least it's easy if their lists are a match to the kind of event you're promoting. If you invite someone to speak at your event on financial planning and their list consists of gardeners, you probably won't get anyone to respond or attend. If, on the other hand, these are people who have requested information on asset protection, there is a good chance the mailing will bring in registrations.

Money from their product sales

Using other speakers will also allow you to generate more cash. Most speakers you ask to speak will have products to sell. If they don't, you'll want to have other very compelling reasons to invite them.

When I do events, I like to make sure that about half of the speakers have products to sell. The others need to be great speakers. I then try to alternate the two. I try to avoid having two speakers back to back who sell product. I also try to avoid having two speakers who are quite good but who may not offer products for sale.

Cons

Unpredictability

You never know how an outside speaker **might** behave or what kinds of stunts they might pull. I've seen a speaker go nuts up in front of a group. This can severely jeopardize your event.

Prima Donnas

A lot of people are extremely difficult to deal with. They make all sorts of demands and are not "team players." I know one very well known speaker who has been silently banned by seminar promoters due to his difficult nature. Ask other people who have used a proposed speaker at their event before you invite him or her to your event.

Bad Speakers

There are plenty of bad speakers. You don't want them speaking at your events. Some people have such great content that you can tolerate a poor speaker. If you do this, just don't use too many who would fall into this category.

Financial Arrangements

There are a number of models for the financial relationship between you and outside speakers you invite to your events.

One way is a straight split of product sales with no expenses paid. Savvy speakers will agree to this when there will be plenty of people in attendance **and** when they are good at product sales. Other speakers will accept this deal if they are anxious to get practice or exposure.

In this first scenario, your speakers will be pretty annoyed if you don't pack the house. Speakers that show up paying their own way expect a decent-sized audience to be able to make it up in product sales. Make sure to manage their expectations by underestimating the number of people you think you'll have in attendance. It's better to have them pleasantly surprised than disappointed.

A second option is to pay their expenses to come to your event and then you split the proceeds of their product sales 50-50. This arrangement is generally used when the people you invite to speak are in demand as speakers. A slight variation on this arrangement would be one in which you agree to let the speaker cover their expenses by keeping the first product sales proceeds until their expenses are met. After that point, you split the proceeds 50-50.

The third type of arrangement is to give speakers some kind of a minimum guarantee. You might use this approach where potential speakers are unsure about what attendance at your event will be. However, do not agree to this arrangement without having seen the speaker in action in front of another group. Never make a guarantee of $3,000 without doing due diligence to find out whether you are making a good decision. This works if you have enough people to get the numbers and a speaker who knows how to sell their stuff when they are up in front of the group.

The final way that some people get outside speakers is by paying their speakers a flat fee. Sometimes a really great speaker might be paid a flat fee and still be allowed to keep all the proceeds of product sales. But that should be a very rare occurrence, particularly in the early going for your seminar business.

There are certain celebrity speakers who will expect to be compensated for speaking at your events. In general, I'm not in favor of paying these folks to speak. The reason is simple. Most of the time it doesn't make economic sense.

The whole area of speaker compensation is fraught with danger. Here's a real-life example to illustrate that point.

A seminar presenter contacted me about an event he was about to hold in the New York City area. I suggested that he mail to my list of people who have attended my workshops in that area.

The deal I offered him was that we would split the registration revenue from my in-house list equally and that he would also give me a speaking slot at his event, where I'd pay my own expenses and sell my own products. He refused both. He wanted me to rent his list. This just isn't how it works in the seminar business, so I refused.

I'm a pretty damn good speaker and he had people who he "allowed" to speak at this event that were average compared to me.

After the event, I heard from a reliable source that this guy lost close to $30,000 on this event. I frankly don't know if that number is correct. But, his response to the disaster was to claim that it was good for his "positioning." Positioning for what, I asked? **Bankruptcy**?

What's In It For Them Besides Money?

Some speakers haven't got the Fred Gleeck message yet and are not (yet!) big into product sales. Some of these speakers will agree to speak for you in response to the "exposure" argument. This is a bogus argument in my opinion, but many speakers will go for that pitch. Tell them how they will get plenty of it by speaking at your event.

Another reason people may want to speak at an event for no fee is to practice their speaking skills. This is dangerous. Let them do their practicing at someone else's event.

Some speakers who are financially secure speak at events to be able to hang out with their friends in the industry. If you are in that position, it's a serious reason to do these events.

For some speakers, there might be real value in just learning from your event, either about the industry you're in or about speaking. This is particularly true of people who are not necessarily in the beginner class but who might still be honing their skills and knowledge.

Of course, another thing speakers who work free might be interested in is adding some of your customers to their databases. That's OK. As long as you stay better than your competition and don't generally invite competitors to speak, you'll be fine.

Locating Speakers

There are three primary ways you can find speakers for your events.

Many times, people you know will be happy to speak at your event as a favor or in return for you speaking at their event. Chances are there are plenty of people in your personal network who have knowledge in the field your seminar covers. Just ask. As any good salesman knows, until you ask, the answer is no.

Another way is to find them on the Web. Go to a search engine and type in key words describing the subject matter for your seminar. Visit the Web sites that come up and do some snooping around. This will give you an idea of who the person is. If they seem like a possible "player," contact them and see if they'd be interested.

There are some good Web sites for starting points, too. Try places like About.com (www.about.com) Experts.com (www.experts.com), Yahoo! Experts (experts.yahoo.com, or refdesk.com (www.refdesk.com/expert.html), which provides dozens of links to sites where experts hang out.

You might also find a speaker at an event that you attend where you see them speak. Approach them after they do their presentation and ask them for some time either right there on the spot or over the phone at a later date.

You can also find people who advertise in the trade publications within your niche or someone the organization might recommend.

Speakers NOT to Invite

There are certain people who you don't want to have speak at your events. They are the people who won't be happy no matter what you do or how the event turns out. You can generally get a good idea as to how they will behave when you talk to them. Even if you're sure they aren't that way, check references on any new speaker you don't know, even if they have a national reputation.

I have been in the seminar business for a long time. I hear a lot of stories about other speakers. Many of them aren't very encouraging. You can call my office if you have a question about a specific speaker and I'll give you my opinion or experience if I have any.

How to Treat Your Speakers

Treat your speakers well, particularly if you're not compensating them. Have a special get-together the night before the event for them. Buy them dinner. Give them a nice gift when they're done. Treat them like what they are ... invited guests.

Yeah, I know this is just common sense and politeness. But you'd be surprised how often I've seen this advice not followed. If you already know and do this, great. If you have ever been treated badly by someone else whose event you spoke at, at least now you know that is not the general rule!

Testing Your Seminar

You must test to know what does and doesn't work. As Declan Dunn, a colleague and a friend, says: "There are only two types of businesses, those that test and those that lose money."

I couldn't agree more.

Always test small before rolling out. It's always better to make a small mistake than a big one.

Once you're convinced you have a winner, roll it out slowly just to make sure. If a seminar works in Pittsburgh, it may not work in Jackson, Mississippi.

Test in every way you can think of before spending the big bucks to promote nationally or internationally.

Online testing is easier and faster than offline testing. You can easily do what are called A-B tests where you send half of an email list one offer or presentation and the other half of the list an alternative idea and measure precisely the results as they come back. And they come back quickly.

You can even test whether a particular concept is a good one before you build the product. How? Go to one of the pay-per-click search engines like GoTo.com and look for the key words that describe your planned product or topic. You can pay a few cents per click-through in many cases and put an upper spending limit in place. Then you can track how many people click on the link when they find it in the search engine and how many of those respond positively to your offer. With a very small investment ($200 or less in most cases) you can find out whether your offer is compelling and what percentage of people who find out about it are likely to buy it. This is very important information to obtain so easily.

If this idea intrigues you, call and ask me for the six hours of audio-taped interview I did with one of the most successful online marketers in the world, Yanik Silver.

Creating the Supporting Product Line

Why You Need Supporting Products

Did you know that most people who conduct seminars, bootcamps, and workshops earn as much or more money from the products their attendees buy on-site as they do from the seminars themselves?

Did you know that people who have only a book to offer earn less than one-third as much as other authors who have a supporting product line for the book?

Those are both true statements. And they explain why you need a line of products that support your seminar or workshop. The answer is simple: more money. As I've said before, I'm interested in maximizing your revenue as a seminar presenter. Absolutely the best way to do that is to have a line of products you sell from the podium at the back of the room. Without it, you're giving up piles of money.

The Product Funnel

It's easy enough to say that you need a product line. But how do you plan and produce a product *line*? What does it mean to have a line of products as opposed to a product or just a bunch of products? I believe your best chance for success in the supporting (or back-end) product area is to fill as many positions in what I call the "Product Funnel" as you can.

Over the years, I've created my own version of the famed Product Funnel. Picture in your mind a funnel. Coming in the top of the funnel are prospects. You obtain these through all the lead-generating techniques we'll talk about in Chapters 7 and 8. Every prospect who buys something purchases what for that customer we can call the front end product. The vast majority of your first-time buyers will purchase something from you that represents low risk, high potential return, and gives them a chance to get to know you as an information provider.

Once you have converted a prospect into a customer by selling him or her anything, the Product Funnel concept comes into play. You want to sell that person one copy of every product in the funnel. To do this, you'll use a technique called "upselling" which involves convincing a customer to buy the next higher-priced item in your product line. Once they've done that, they become a candidate for the next higher-priced item. And so it goes.

This is not to say that some people won't come into your product funnel at the highest price point (for example, a consulting gig) and then buy other, *lower*-priced products. Nor is it to imply that someone who comes in at, say, a $30 price point (by buying your book, for example), isn't going to leap right up and become a consulting client or buy into your expensive three-day bootcamp. But *most* of your customers will tend to enter the funnel at a reasonable price point (under $50 as a rule) and then be willing to buy up in price as they get to know you and the quality of your work.

I recommend that you define and create products at least at the following approximate price levels as you design and fill out your product line:

- $10 or less (a special report, excerpt from a book, special issue of a newsletter, research study)
- $20-40 (typically a book; we'll talk shortly about why having a book is such an important idea for you as a seminar leader)
- $100-$200 (audio or video cassette collection or, in some cases, individual training videos)
- $300-$500 (one-day seminar or perhaps a seminar-workshop or a half-day workshop)
- $600-$1,000 (bootcamp or multi-day intensive seminar/workshop)

If you follow this formula and then design a careful tracking and followup system (using email autoresponders at your online store is easily the best way to accomplish this, particularly if some portion of your product line can be made electronically deliverable), I can guarantee you that you'll see increased income.

Make Your Products Specific

The more specific you make your products, the higher the prices you can charge for them. Also, the more specific they are, the easier it will be to sell them. Why?

Here's a story to illustrate. If I were selling a generic marketing program for small business I might be able to charge $99, but for the self-storage industry I can charge $297 and people don't bat an eye. Why? Specificity. People who are in the self-storage industry will know (or believe) that they are going to get very specifically targeted help with their very specific problems from a seminar aimed at them. I might provide essentially the same information in such a seminar as I would, say, for people in the catering industry. But by carefully selecting examples, experts to cite, statistics to back up points, and in-class exercises to focus on their specific industry, I can create a highly targeted product, 80% or more of which is generic to all such products in my catalog.

I recently recorded a program with another speaker for just one gig in a niche market of mine. He is an expert in customer service and I know the specific industry. We recorded a program together and he ended up selling over $8,000 worth of products that I'm sure he wouldn't have without the custom program we did.

He had over 1,200 people together for a keynote speech, so it was worth it. Now, that program can be sold for the next 3 to 5 years in that industry and continue to make money both of us.

Overcoming Your Perfectionist Bent

You can spend a lifetime trying to make your product perfect. Trust me, they will never be perfect! Do the best you can do and get it out there. With all of the money you make from this first round of products you can always improve them. If you feel guilty about this, send the people who bought the first product an offer to buy the new program at cost or slightly above cost. This will build a lot of good will and alleviate your guilt.

There's another good reason not to strive for perfection in your product line. Customers who have good ideas about how to improve your product will come to you with those suggestions and you can continue to upgrade your quality. If you have a program that doesn't leave room for improvement, you eliminate a channel of communication with your customers.

Getting That Book Written

As you have undoubtedly figured out by now, I'm a strong advocate of you publishing a book in your area of expertise as a major component of success in the seminar business. There are a number of reasons for this, but here are the most important and obvious.

First, a book is a marvelous credibility-builder. Nothing gives you instant credibility like having authored a book on a topic. We all know the expression "He wrote the book on that." It gets used lots of places where people didn't write a book at all, but have become the acknowledged experts by virtue of their long experience.

Second, a book makes a terrific front-end product. Its price point (generally in the $20-50 range) is sufficiently low that new customers will be relatively willing to give you a credit card to purchase it (as opposed, for example, to a $300 seminar) without having to know much more about you than that you wrote it.

Third, a book is an amazing entree to a conversation. I once found myself on an airplane with a person who turned out to be a prospect for my consulting business. He asked if I had a card. "No," I said, "but how would you like a copy of my book?" That blew him away.

Fourth, a book *can* be a good source of revenue if it's marketed right. (We're not going to go into marketing books in this book, but if you're interested, you should look at my program, *Publishing for Maximum Profit.*)

Now that I have convinced you that you *need* a book, what do you do next? If you are a good writer and are comfortable with the process of writing a book-length manuscript, just do it! Write the book. Self-publish it. Shamelessly promote it. Build a product line around it.

But what if, like most people, you have never written a book, aren't sure of the process, or perhaps aren't even comfortable writing much of anything (like me)? There's hope!

You should get in touch with my friend and partner Dan Shafer at Publishing Profit, Inc. (dan@publishingprofit.com) and check out his services. He can help you in any (or all) of three ways.

First, he can personally ghost-write your book for you or assign your book to one of his professional freelance writing associates at Publishing Profit. Your personal ghost writer interviews you, gathers other written or taped information you have, follows your additional research leads, and outlines the book. After you've signed off on the Table of Contents, the writer produces the manuscript for you.

The book has your name as author. As far as the world's concerned, you wrote it.

Second, he can have one of Publishing Profit's outstanding team of editors review your draft manuscript and polish it into shape as a book. This can include not only reviewing and editing your material and, if necessary, organizing it, but also suggesting ways to lengthen the book if it's too short, pointing out content that might be missing, and otherwise working with the manuscript as a book in process.

Finally, Dan takes on a limited number of clients to coach their writing skills. These people work on their own projects and get a weekly phone consultation with him during which they can get answers to tough questions, solve writers' block problems, get additional training in areas where they may be weak, and discuss project progress.

Creating Audios

Audio tapes are the easiest products to create. If you told me you needed to have products within a week, I could help you put together a few different sets of audio tapes that might sell for as much as $500.

There are at least three ways to create these products.

First, you can record a live seminar. If you do this, make sure the audience is well miked. Doing products this way creates a product that has a lot of energy.

Another way to do them is to create an extensive outline and have someone interview you. I recently did this for a client and we created a six-hour audio program that he can sell for $195. He'll be able to sell it for a few years and we project a minimum of $250,000 in revenue.

Your third option is to interview experts in the field. This can be done face to face or by phone. Most experts will agree to this arrangement in exchange for you including their contact information. If you lined up six experts and interviewed them back to back on one day you could have a program done in a day. Similarly, this could sell for $195. Or you might interview one expert for six hours, reversing the role I described in the previous paragraph.

The last option is to go into the studio and basically talk into a mike. I don't care who you are, this is tough to pull off. Tony Robbins is one of the few people who could do this and make it work. I still have a hard time with his stuff. It's tough to keep someone's interest for very long as a solo act with no audience interaction.

You don't need a fancy, expensive recording machine when you get started. But, you do need to get started! A good place to start is my audio program, "Creating and Selling Information Products," about which you can find information in Appendix A.

Creating Videos

Video tapes are great products to include in your Product Funnel. You can make a lot more money with videos than with any other form of product. But please don't try to put together your own video product without guidance. The process isn't overly complex but until you have some experience, there are dozens of pitfalls to avoid. Only experience helps you learn to do these well.

I've done hundreds of video projects. Give me a call and I'll give you my thoughts. I can help you figure out a good process for creating them and I can get you in touch with the right people to help you.

Publishing a Newsletter or eZine

If you have information that changes frequently or if you are able to dig up little tidbits of information regularly that will enlighten your customers and make their businesses more successful, you should consider publishing an email newsletter or an eZine (electronic magazine). The primary difference between the two is that an email newsletter is generally produced entirely in plain text and emailed to people, while an eZine is more like a Web site that includes graphics, nice layouts, headlines, etc., and your customers come to it. (It is, however, possible to use HTML email to send out an eZine, though many people use email programs that don't understand HTML and can't do anything with the gibberish they receive in that case.)

Even if you do an email newsletter, you will want to pay attention to little techniques that make it more readable, attractive, and helpful.

One good thing about both of these forms of communication is that they give you an excuse to stay in regular contact with your customer base. Another good thing is that both can contain hyperlinks on which your customer/reader/prospect can click and be transported to your Web site where you get a chance to make a more detailed sales pitch for a specific product, service, or special offer.

Don't give these things away just to get names into your database, though. This is one of what Web marketing guru Yanik Silver calls a myth: that you have to give something away on the Web to get people to pay attention to your offerings. Either this newsletter or eZine has value for which your customers are willing to pay or you probably shouldn't bother with it in the first place.

(An exception to that might be that you *include* a newsletter subscription as a premium when they purchase another product of yours. This is often a very attractive marketing and pricing strategy. Several well-known seminar leaders have relatively costly monthly newsletters but give attendees at their seminars a free one-year subscription.)

Pricing Your Products

I can't tell you how to price your products, of course. You have to learn your market's expectations and sensitivity points by experience and research. But I can and will offer you some general guidelines for pricing that prove true across a broad range of products and industries.

Always offer people an A, B, or C option. What the price points are for each of these options depends on the market you're in. If you're selling to plastic surgeons, the numbers will be significantly higher than if you're selling to caterers.

Let's take an "average" example. I would suggest you price one package at around $100. Price your package "B" at around $300 and package "C" at around $700. Play with these numbers in your market to see what works best. But, that's a good place to start.

If you have a book, **never** sell it alone. It gives people too easy a way out when they want to buy something but aren't sure what. They give you the $25 and they're done. Instead use your book as a premium for anyone who buys one or more of your packages (A, B or C).

Depending on your attendees, you may want to adjust your prices upwards or downwards. I have a standard order sheet in one of my markets. It lists three packages. Package A goes for $397. Package B goes for $597 and package C goes for $997.

When I start my pitch from the podium during a seminar, I tell them to strike through the $397 price and put $297. Then I have them strike through the $597 price and put $497. I mark the C package price down to $777. Maybe I've been in Las Vegas too long, but that's what I do.

If I've got a group that I feel can afford it, I may only knock $50 off each of the smaller packages and $100 off the large package. It all depends on the group and what I think they will "tolerate." If you have a multi-day event, you can always go back and cut prices some more if they don't buy.

Again, this is more of an art than a science. Test things for yourself. Email me and tell me how it worked out.

Packaging Your Products

Make your life simple and come up with standard packaging for your products. Try to have no more than two or three different packages. Trust me, I've done it the other way and it becomes an incredible nightmare.

Create packaging that looks good, but isn't overly slick. If you make your product packaging look **too** good it makes people wonder about how good the content is. Simple but attractive is probably the best way to describe what I'd recommend.

Remember, it's about selling the greatest amount of product, not creating packaging that will win awards.

When you cut the prices of your products you have to do it for a reason. If you don't, people will wonder why you didn't cut the prices even more.

The best way I've found to do this effectively is to offer the products with little or no packaging. That way I can say to people that the reason I can cut $100 off the cost of the package is they get the stuff wrapped in rubber bands.

This has proved incredibly effective. Most people who do seminars will cut prices without any logical explanation. Doing things the way I suggest not only cuts your costs, it makes the price breaks that you give buyers make sense.

Future Product Ideas

Today, audio and video tapes of any significant length must be sold as a physical product. These could be in the form of an audio tape, a video tape, or a CD-ROM. Books can now be delivered digitally in eBook form.

In the future, audio and video will be more broadly deliverable digitally as well. Given current technology, delivering an audio program of six hours in length (or even an hour) over the internet is impractical. This won't be true forever. In the not-too-distant future, we'll be delivering audio and video content via the Web.

When that happens, profit margins will go through the roof. We won't have to pay to duplicate the tapes and shipping costs will disappear.

Keep an eye on the technology developments that are making this form of delivery increasingly possible. Get your content into digital form so that you can take advantage of online delivery when it's feasible. (Digital media also stores more reliably and doesn't fade or decay over time, so it's always good to have a digital master of your content somewhere anyway.)

Should You Sell Other Peoples' Products?

If you don't have your own products to sell at this point, then by all means sell someone else's. If you like mine, give me a call and we'll set you up as a dealer. The split is 50-50 and we do the shipping, for which the buyer pays. Many people in the seminar business will make similar deals with you.

But you want to develop your own product line as soon as possible. Not only will this be more profitable, but you can control the content, quality, and referral business that grows from the products.

There may still be some products that you won't want to create yourself. Someone else may have the greatest product in the world on that topic and you don't want to try to improve on it. If that's the case, don't. Just sell the other person's product in addition to your own.

The Product Line's Supporting Cast

Testimonials

Testimonials are an extremely effective method of selling anything, not the least of which are your products. Every once in a while you'll have someone stand up in your seminar and give you an unsolicited testimonial for your products. Thank them and try to appear a little embarrassed. Then, later, ask them if they'd mind saying the same thing on tape and/or in a signed letter or fax.

If you have testimonials, you can also read those. These tend to be most effective if people can see that they are real. Bring the ones that are written on a person's letterhead and let the audience see that you are reading an actual letter.

Having Bags With Your Name On Them

You'll need to get some bags with your name and phone number printed on them. If you work (like I do) in a number of different markets you'll want to make them generic enough to be used in different niches.

My bags say: "Fred Gleeck's Marketing Magic Success System" and provide my 800 number at the bottom. Doing them this way allows me to use them with any market I deal with. I don't have to have several different bags.

If you are **sure** you're only going to be doing work in one industry, there might be some value in making your bags more specific. If not, follow my lead and make them generic.

Giving a Guarantee

I offer a lifetime guarantee on everything I sell. This includes products and seminars. I suggest you do the same. When I get up in front of a group to pitch my products, I make a stronger offer than I had made before they got to the seminar. I tell them that unless they get at least 10 times what they paid for the package, they should send it all back.

My experience is that if you have good-quality products and seminars and you are confident in them, you will find that very few people ever ask for a refund. You might even learn something valuable from the few who do.

*L*etting Them Know You Have a Seminar
(Marketing 101)

Pricing Your Event to Maximize Revenue

Pricing is an important piece of the revenue maximization puzzle. Up to a point, the lower you price the seminar, the more people will attend. Where's that point? You may be tired of hearing the answer by now, but it stays the same: test your market! One thing we do know: a free seminar will **always** be perceived as a sales pitch even though you don't intend it to be one.

This will give you more opportunities to sell your products. Right? Maybe! When you price the seminar too low you might attract attendees who can't afford to buy your products.

If you price the seminar too high you won't attract enough people who might buy your products. What's the answer? **Test**!

In my tests of a number of my markets I have found the $297 price to be the right one for a one-day seminar. Please don't take this number and simply assume it will work for you. It may. It may not. **Test**!

The way I determine the right price is by computing the total number of dollars that come in from the seminar as a result of a given price. I found that at $99 for that same seminar people didn't buy much product. They also were pains in the ass to deal with. Very little consulting business resulted. This was obviously not the right price.

I then tried $495. I got a lot fewer people at the seminar. They didn't buy all that much more product than the group who paid $99. Some of the people became consulting clients. Price optimization for me in this particular market occurs at $297. It seems to give me the best of everything.

The only way for you to find out what price is right for you is to test for yourself. Call me to discuss what price you may want to start at.

The more specific your seminar, the higher the prices you can charge. If I'm doing a generic marketing seminar for small business people I might be able to charge $100. If I'm doing a marketing seminar for caterers or self storage operators, I can easily charge $300 for a one-day marketing seminar customized to that niche.

How you price your seminars is a very important factor in determining your overall profitability. But if your goal is the maximization of revenue, you need to need to consider revenue generated from seminar registration as just one of the components. Remembering the formula: **TR = SR + PS + CB** you can see that seminar registration is just one of the three components in computing total revenue. If you look at CB (consulting business) as gravy, then you only have two components to consider.

Let's look at three possible prices for a seminar. Let's take a one-day seminar and price it at $497. Assuming this is a market that normally expects to pay between $200 and $300 for a one-day seminar we are quite a bit on the high side.

You might expect to get fewer registrations at this price point. If we take consulting business off the table, let's look at product sales. Clearly, people who are willing to pay $497 for a one day event are eminently qualified to buy our products. Here's the problem. Although they are qualified, there will probably be fewer people in the room.

With fewer people in the room there will be less of a "feeding frenzy" when you make your product offer. As a result, the mob mentality will be reduced and by virtue of this fact alone, you may not close as many sales.

Also, people who paid that amount may be reluctant to shell out additional dollars to buy products, feeling that they have spent all they should for this event.

Let's jump to the other side of the pricing equation. Let's say you charged $97. You would get a lot more people to register. If we once again take CB off the table, let's explore what **might** happen to PS. Since there are more people, we may get more sales. However, since the entry price is so low, this group might be the type who are reluctant to spend any money at all for product sales.

At this $97 price point, if we could get a few people to buy, it might create a buying frenzy and that would be good.

At the mid-point price of $297, we might maximize the total registration dollars and also have a group who would be willing to buy products. Given that the price was low enough, there might also be enough people to create a "minor" frenzy. Overall, this mid-point price might maximize TR.

All the above being said, there is only one way to know what price to charge for your events — **test**! If you don't test, you'll never know. Testing will make it easy for you to optimize your price because you'll be dealing in reality rather than fantasy.

From the above discussion **do not** assume I am suggesting you price your one day seminars at or around $300. I don't know what will work for you and wouldn't hazard a guess! You don't know what price optimization would be until you test. When you test, make sure to include only TR & PS in your computation.

I would speculate that the higher-priced registrants, everything else being equal, would be more likely to buy your consulting services. But this is purely speculation. The only way to find out for certain is to test. The problem with testing is that you will not get any immediate results as it relates to the CB component.

From experience, I can tell you that if you compared the low, medium and high price points for a seminar, you would probably find that those who paid the low registration fee would be **much** less likely to give you consulting business. That has been my experience over time. Your mileage may vary.

Whichever price point you choose, give people an incentive for early enrollment. My experience — and again you need to **test** your markets to see if this experience has value for you — is that if I give people a 10% discount for registering more than 2 weeks before the event, it increases sales without reducing revenue appreciably and takes away some of the stomach-wrenching fear of a seminar failing.

Some seminar promoters use a two-step seminar promotion method. This is where they offer a free seminar and heavily promote it. They use this free event to sell people into a higher-priced weekend seminar the following weekend. This has been very effective in the real estate market and in some others I have both heard and seen.

Again, testing is the only way to know what works. If you're a good salesperson for your seminar, this can be a highly effective way of doing things.

Promoting the Seminar

Testimonials: The "Mother's Milk" of Seminar Promotion

By far the most effective means of selling your seminar are testimonials from previous seminar attendees. The best time to capture these testimonials is at the event itself. This is when people are the most "lathered up" about your event and most inclined to give you a glowing report.

You'll want to get them in written form, which is best accomplished through the use of an evaluation form where you ask people to sign the form after they jot down some words of praise. When you hand out your evaluations , instruct people to give you **specific** comments. A general, watered-down testimonial is virtually useless.

You may even want to coach them a bit on what you're looking for by giving an example. I always tell people: "If you think your profits will double as a result of using the hotline, please put that down."

When you speak to people after your event and they tell you great things that have happened as a result of your event, quickly ask them if you can write up what they said and fax it over to them for their signature. Again, the key is to strike while the iron is hot. If they have great things to say, get them in writing.

I also recommend that you keep the video camera rolling towards the end of your event and get people to give you video testimonials. You'll be able to use them in a variety of ways to help you promote future events. You can send out videos or stream them from your Web site. You can also choose to use only the audio portion of the testimonial.

Public Relations

Publicity can be a very effective way to promote your event. This is particularly true if you do it yourself. Paying a PR person can be expensive and often times won't pull enough responses to justify the costs.

There are three pieces to the publicity puzzle as it relates to your seminars. First, you want to get the coverage. Second, you want to do the best job you can once you're in front of the media. Lastly, you want to sell a lot of seminar seats with this opportunity.

To generate publicity, you'll need a hook. This is what causes the media to want to cover your event. You'll also want to formulate your message. This is what you say once you're in front of the media.

An important thing to remember is that there are tons of people who are trying to get in front of the media to help promote their seminar or event. The media gets bombarded with requests for coverage from seminar promoters. This means that you must have something newsworthy or unusual to get their attention.

In many cases, you'll be doing the publicity yourself. This is nothing to be ashamed of. Many people do their own publicity and promotion. If you understand the process, you can be very successful. Who can be a better advocate for your seminar or event than you?

Media Coaching Can Help

Before you start getting in front of the media, it's a good idea to understand how the process works. This will allow you to optimize your opportunities. I'd recommend that you go to a seminar by Joel Roberts to find out exactly how to maximize your chances for success.

I have spent some time with Joel and attended his seminars. He does a great job in this area. Contact either Joel or his assistant Nancy. Let him know I sent you. You'll be glad you did. (His contact information is in the Million-Dollar Rolodex in Appendix A.)

Using Outside Publicity Experts

There are many people who present themselves as publicity experts who will be happy to take your money in exchange for claiming to help you promote your event. Be suspicious.

If a publicity person is confident he or she can get you publicity, I suggest you compensate them differently than they might prefer. Offer to give them a piece of all of the registrations that come in from their efforts. Let's say the seminar is priced at $300. Let's also assume that the marginal cost for each attendee is $25. This means that every registration is worth $275 (net) to you.

Offer your publicity person a minimum of a 50-50 split on the registration dollars for every person that their efforts generate. (This assumes that you can track the responses.)

I would even consider giving them more. If necessary, I'll give a PR person $200 for each person their efforts can generate. I'll still make $75 on the front end and have the opportunity to sell them products and other services while I build a larger database.

Most PR people will balk at this deal. Fine. Only use people who are willing to bite at this arrangement. If they are really good, they'll actually make a lot more money.

Persistence Pays

The key to getting media coverage is to be persistent. Don't expect to make one call and have them asking you to sit down for an interview and a photo shoot. As with all things where you're relying on someone else to do something that's higher on your list than it is on theirs, persistence is the key here. Without being a pest, regular and polite call-backs are in order. If you've left several messages and none are being returned, a final message that simply says, "I assume you're not interested and I don't want to keep pestering you, so I'm not going to call again. But if you are interested and just busy right now, please do call me as soon as you can and let's talk about how we can help each other" is definitely appropriate.

If you're easily discouraged when people seem to ignore you, you'll find the PR route tough sledding. Editors are not only busy people, they are suspicious as well. Press releases tend not to get the kind of attention that the people who send them think they deserve. But if you are gently persistent in your follow-up, you can often get a reporter or editor on the phone to talk to you about your story. It's more often that conversation, rather than the release itself, that will lead to coverage.

So don't give up and don't get discouraged!

Don't Be Hurt When They Don't Cover You

When, despite your patience and persistence, you don't get coverage by the media, don't be discouraged and don't take it personally. These folks are just doing their jobs. Your goal is to make your event so enticing that they are compelled to give you coverage.

Sometimes you just don't have a newsworthy event. It's not likely any major metropolitan daily newspaper or TV outlet or radio show is going to cover your seminar unless it has a hook and is something they haven't seen before (or at least recently). No hook, no coverage, even on a slow news day.

The Hook

The hook is what causes the media to stop what they're doing and take notice of your event. If there has just been an earthquake in San Francisco and you're doing a seminar on how to earthquake-proof your house, you've got a relatively easy sell.

In most cases, things won't be this easy.

You can also take a specific portion of your seminar and try to create a hook. In order for your hook to be effective you'll want to try and tie it to some current event or trend in the field.

TV Publicity (Empty)

We live in a time that is dominated by television. It's only natural that you would be eager to get yourself some good TV publicity. Don't bother. As good as seeing your face on TV may be for your ego, stations rarely let you put up an 800 number or a Web site URL. This makes TV appearances just about worthless for product promotion unless you're already known and people can find you easily. I recommend that you not pursue TV unless you know someone.

Radio

To learn how to get your event covered on radio, I suggest you learn from the master of the radio interview, Alex Carroll. He has done more interviews for one book than virtually anyone on the planet.

Go to his site, www.radiopublicity.com, to learn more about him and some of the materials that he has to offer. His information is backed by real-life experience as the interviewee in well over 1,000 radio interviews.

Print

The master of print publicity is another friend of mine, Paul Hartunian. Paul has generated the equivalent of well over $6 million in space advertising in magazines and newspapers. I suggest you obtain his materials before you start promoting your own events.

Give me a call and we'll get you a set of his materials.

Online

There are a number of sources for you to generate on-line publicity.

Some of these depend on your topic. If you're giving a seminar of interest to the building trades industry, for example, you should use your favorite search engine (my technical colleague Dan Shafer, who's a real guru in this field, currently recommends www.google.com) and look up building trades sites. Some, particularly associations and eZines devoted to your space, will be happy to list your seminar free.

You can also post notices about your seminars and workshops on the email lists, listservs, and discussion boards you belong to and contribute to regularly. Be careful here; spam is not appreciated and can have a severe negative side effect. But if you're a regular member of and contributor to some online communities in your space, and if you're careful about how you promote your seminar (avoiding blatant, obvious promotions but perhaps including a line about your upcoming seminar in your personal sig line, for example), you can often get peoples' attention here.

Joint Venture Mailings

Email Joint Ventures

The best way to promote your events is by doing joint venture email marketing. Identify others who have email lists that you feel would be responsive to your seminar offer and then ask the list owner e-mail either your promotion or a link to your Web site. You split your profit with them in return for their help.

You can find people with whom to do these joint ventures by scouring the Web for sites that rank high on the search engines or get a lot of traffic and whose audience has something in common with yours. Sometimes, these sites are competitive to yours and in many of those cases, the site owners may not want to help you become more successful.

You generally split the gross registration fee profit with joint venture partners 50-50. Let's say you have an event for which you're charging $997 and on which you have hard costs of about $30 per attendee. You would give a joint venture partner about $480 for every person who registers from their list or site. Why so much? It gives your joint venture partners a reason for doing the deal **and** it only costs you $30 out of pocket for each additional person.

This is a great way to promote because you put no money up front. Also, if you have a decent back end the lifetime value of these new-found customers could be considerable. (Remember that once they sign up for your seminar or product, they are no longer exclusive property of your joint venture partner.)

This is my preferred way to promote seminars. If you use this method exclusively, you can break even with even a tiny number of total registrations.

Direct-Mail Joint Ventures

Despite the clear advantages of email marketing, many seminars are still being promoted via direct mail. I recommend that you move away from direct mail as your primary means of marketing. Why? The cost of printing and postage make it more difficult for you to recover your money.

But if you are going to go the direct-mail route, explore joint-ventured physical mailings. The arrangements here can be many and varied. The person whose list you are mailing to is concerned about the integrity of their list.

You will usually compose the letter, pay for the mailing and then give the mailing list owner a per-name fee or a percentage based on response.

With the right list, this can be a very effective way to promote your event. Given the incredibly high costs associated with this type of a mailing, however, you'll want to test the list before mailing the entire lot.

The nice thing about using this technique is that once people respond, they become a part of your in-house list. If your lifetime customer value is high, it might even make sense to use this method of promotion if you can only achieve a break-even on the front end.

You can also rent various types of mailing lists both on and off line to promote your seminar or event. Generally, this method does not pay off. Perhaps the biggest reason: a seminar priced higher than $100 or so requires that people know who you are. Unless you have some celebrity in the field, a blind mailing to a list of people who have a specific profile won't likely sell anything with a very high price tag.

Third-Party Online Newsletters

There are two ways of looking at online newsletters as promotional aids for your seminar: buying advertising space or obtaining free publicity or even an endorsement.

My success using on-line **ads** to promote seminars is abysmal. (This, of course, parallels just about everyone's experience with online advertising in general.) I would only work with on-line newsletters if they write a little article or endorse my event.

Your experience may be different. If so, please contact me and share your experience. From my own experience, it isn't cost effective.

The only successful way to work on-line is through joint-venture emailing, which is described above.

Paid Advertising

Advertising R.O.M.D.

R.O.M.D. is an acronym for "Return on Marketing Dollar." To understand this concept, you'll need some important background information. Every advertising and promotional method you use will have a different level of effectiveness. The only way to find out your precise numbers will be through testing. But here is a blueprint for how things will almost certainly work.

Let's say your seminar is priced at $300. Let's also say that your marginal cost for each additional attendee is $25. Marginal cost is the actual "hard cost" of having an additional person in attendance. This would include the cost of your handouts, drinks, meals or any other cost that would increase if another person came to your event.

Knowing that every additional person costs you $25 allows you to proceed with your computations.

Let's say that your newspaper ad will cost you $2,000 and it ends up generating 10 attendees. Would your R.O.M.D be 1:3 ($2,000: $6,000)? No. You need to add on marginal cost of having the 10 people. Adding on $250 (10 x $25) you get $2250. So your true R.O.M.D. is $2250:$6000. This works out to 1: 2.66.

The rule of thumb is that even if you only break even on a marketing approach, you should consider using it since it doesn't take into account back-of-the-room sales. Since the ratio in this case is greater than 1:1, you would use the newspaper ad with some confidence. In cases where you had a history of high product sales, you may even use those marketing methodologies that produced R.O.M.D. ratios that are slightly less than 1:1.

Since we already know that TR = SR + PS + CB, we know that you make money "on the front end" with any marketing method that produces a ratio of greater than 1:1. If you're just starting out in the seminar business, stick with those marketing methods that produce a minimum of 1:1 ratios.

If you have a history of doing this seminar, your computations will be different. If you "know" that the average customer will generate an additional $150 in product sales, we can compute the ratio including the product sales number.

In this example, spending $2,250 will produce $3,000 (SR) + $1,500 (product sales for 10 people: $150 X 10) for a total of $4,500. In this case, the numbers work out extremely neatly (as you might have guess I planned them). Your R.O.M.D. is 1:2 (2,250: 4,500).

This means that for every dollar you spend on this particular advertising/promotional vehicle you generate $2 in total revenue.

The CB component doesn't come in immediately. Some consulting business that you generate may come in well after the event itself. In my case, I have generated consulting business more than 10 years after a seminar my new client attended.

This being the case, leave the CB component completely out of your computations. Let the consulting business be gravy. Don't use it in your computation of R.O.M.D.

If you included the CB component, you could get yourself into trouble. If you relied on consulting business and it didn't come in (or didn't come in as quickly as you expected) then you might drive yourself bankrupt. Even if the consulting business was significant, you may not be able to handle the cash flow shortfall in the short run.

Unless you can generate a break-even on seminar registration and product sales with a certain method of marketing, don't use it! In essence you have thrown out the "CB" in the equation. You still know that it will bear fruit **eventually**, but for our computations — as well as for your financial peace of mind — leave it out!

Elements of Your Ad or Direct-Mail Piece

Any advertising you do for your seminars will contain virtually all of the same elements. This would apply to ads you place in both newspapers and trade publications. Many of the same elements will also be included in your direct mail pieces.

Here are a list of the elements you'll want to include:

Pre-head: The pre-head is what is at the very top of your ad, usually in fairly small type. It sets the stage for the main headline which is in much larger type. Think of the pre-head as the maitre d for your ad. It introduced people to the headline.

Headline: Your headline is the single most important part of your ad or direct mail piece. The difference between success and failure **could** lie in your headline. You need to work at creating a variety of headlines before settling on one. Some people who do nothing but write this kind of material start out by writing as many as 100 headlines before they start narrowing the selection.

Post Head: This is what comes after the headline and keeps people reading so they enthusiastically read your first paragraph.

Greeting: Your greeting is how you say hello to each individual reader of your direct mail piece. You obviously won't have one of these in your ads.

First Paragraph: Your first paragraph is critical to your success, second only to your headline. You need to suck people in with powerful benefits or they will turn away and do something else with their busy lives.

<u>Testimonials</u>: You wouldn't use the word testimonials as the heading of this section. Instead use something like: "What Others Say About the Seminar." In this section, the more specific the quotation, the better. When identifying the source of the quotation, make sure to include the first and last name as well as the city and state. Also put the name of their company and (if they agree to it) their phone number. The more information you include, the more credible the testimonial will be.

<u>Seminar Fee</u>: Your price or fee should be clear and understandable. How much do people have to pay? What is the deadline to receive the discount? What bonuses do they receive if they respond by what date? Do they get lunch for that fee? All of the typical questions that anyone would want to know should be answered. Also, let them know what methods of payment you accept. Also mention that the fee includes a comprehensive 45-page workbook (or however long it really is).

<u>Unable to Attend</u>?: This section must be included if you're going to generate tape sales. I've heard other marketing gurus suggest that you NOT offer your tapes for sale in your promotional piece for your seminar. I adamantly disagree. I have been doing seminars for quite a while and offering recordings of the live event has never hurt seminar registrations.

If you are offering both video and audio tapes, charge more for the video tapes. Not long ago I forgot to change the prices for the videos and charged the same amount as I do for the audio tapes. This was a mistake. Videos cost a lot more to produce than audios. Make sure you price these items accordingly.

<u>Tax Deductibility</u>: Even though most people know that educational events can be deductible, it doesn't hurt to remind them of the fact.

<u>Limited Attendance</u>: You want to give people the feeling that your event will fill up quickly to encourage them to register promptly. I would suggest specifying a specific number of people that you'll allow to attend. Using this tactic will help to create urgency.

<u>Seminar Hotline</u>: Include a line which says: "For more information call our 24 Hour Free Recorded Seminar Hotline." This should be a separate line that you set up that gives people a verbal pitch of your event. (I discuss hotlines elsewhere in this book.)

<u>Guarantee</u>: An incredibly strong guarantee is a big selling point. You are dealing with a very skeptical public. You have to do any and

everything you can to assuage their fears. A powerful guarantee helps. I offer what I call a "100%, No B.S., No Weasel Clause, Iron Clad, Lifetime Guarantee."

<u>Matching the Typestyle</u>: You'll want to match the typestyle of the publication that you advertise in. The closer you can look like the rest of the publication, the better. Doing this will create an implied endorsement for your event. Some publications realize this and won't let you match their type. Do it until you are instructed that you can't.

<u>Who Should Attend?</u>: This section allows you to target exactly who you want to attend. People reading this section will be looking to find themselves in the group. If they aren't there, they will assume this seminar is not meant for them. List as many different groups as possible as long as the seminar is definitely meant for them.

<u>Early Registration Bonus</u>: Always give people a reason to act **now**. People are always inclined to put things aside and do them later. You have to get them so excited by your seminar offer that they want to sign up immediately. To help move this process along, give them an incentive. This incentive can be a price reduction or some kind of a special free gift. If you use the price reduction, make sure that you put the date by which they must respond to get this special deal.

<u>Your Seminar Leader</u>: In this section, describe yourself and your credentials. You'll want to concentrate on what benefits you have generated for your clients and other attendees of your seminars. Take a look at the samples in Appendix A to give you some ideas.

<u>What You Will Learn (Bullet Points)</u>: This is the most influential section of the main body of your ad. Reading through this section is where most people make a decision about whether or not to attend your event.

<u>Location</u>(s): You'll want to let people know exactly where your event is being held. Give people exact locations and even phone numbers if possible. When there is more than one Hilton in the area, make sure and highlight this fact in the ad and let them know which one it is. Even with these explicit instructions some people will still blow it and go to the other hotel. If your ad is detailed and clear they will blame themselves and not you when they screw up.

<u>Times</u>: Give people the times of your event and when they should be there to register. Tell them they should be there 30–45 minutes in advance to make sure everyone is in by the appointed start time.

<u>Who Should Not Attend?</u>: I've started using this section in trade publications and I feel it works out well. The idea here is to further

sell people on your event using the negative slant. In this section, I tell people who think they know it all or don't want to learn the latest and greatest stuff not to attend. Using this section will also eliminate a lot of jerks who may have attended.

Cancellations: You should have a clearly stated cancellation policy. Even though you offer people an iron-clad guarantee, you should still let people know what to do in the event that they have to cancel.

Newspaper Ads

I started my career in seminars by running space ads in newspapers. I promoted a one-day seminar on a Saturday. I ran the ads the two Sundays before for the following Saturday. When I did my first seminar on Starting Your Own Consulting Business back in the early 80s I spent about $1500 on two 15-inch ads that ran on the two Sundays before my event.

I charged $95 for the seminar and had 44 people show up. I ended up netting around $2,000. I was psyched! The problem is that back then I did not understand the front end/back end concept. I may have made $2000, but I lost a lot more money by not having a decent back-end product line.

I no longer make those mistakes. Live and learn.

The beauty of the newspaper ad as compared with direct mail is that you can decide you want to do a seminar today and three weeks from now be doing a seminar. It shortens the lead time for you to do a seminar.

Of course, email promotion is even faster, but that wasn't an option when I started in this business.

Advertising in newspapers can work well for certain general-interest seminars. The newspaper is a fairly general medium. Since that is the case, it makes sense to test newspaper advertising for seminar topics like making money, losing weight and having better sex. If you have a general seminar topic, you should definitely test the newspaper.

A lot of big cities have two or more major newspapers. Usually only one will work for promoting your seminar. I learned this by mistake many years ago in Dallas. Not being familiar with that city I advertised in the wrong paper. How did I know? I didn't get very many registrations. Luckily, I also did some direct mail, so I squeezed out a small profit.

Before you advertise in a city you know nothing about, talk to people in that city and get their feedback. If I had done this with Dallas, I never would have made the mistake I did.

When you run ads in the main newspaper in a town you'll get calls from various specialty papers. The calls will come from hardworking salespeople trying to sell you advertising space. They will be very convincing in their arguments. Don't bite!

My standard response to an enthusiastic salesperson is to give them a very enthusiastic reply. I say: "It sounds like you think this ad will really work in your publication. Here's what I think we should do. Rather than pay for the space, let's split the revenue 50-50 on all registrations. You can even have the calls come into your office so you can track the responses. That way you can be a partner in this venture and make a lot more money than if I just pay for the space."

After you give them that line, don't say a thing. They will usually have nothing to say. In all the years I have been doing seminars I actually got one publication to go for this scenario. It didn't work out well for either of us, but I didn't spend money up-front to find out. Please follow my lead.

One question that always comes up with newspapers is in which section of the paper to place the ad. This depends on the type of seminar you're doing. I have found that the seminars that I do work best in the main news section of the paper.

It would be very difficult for me to give you specific recommendations in this area without knowing your particular seminar topic. Even if I did know your topic, we would still have to test to see what worked. All the speculation we might do is meaningless. The proof is in the pudding. Test it for yourself to see what works.

When I do a seminar I will occasionally run what are called "tickler ads" a few weeks before the larger ads kick in. These are small (one- or two-inch) ads consisting only of a powerful headline and a phone number to call for more information. If you choose to test these, run a Web site address as well.

It also makes sense to test some classified ads. They are usually extremely affordable and can help to build your mailing list as well as perhaps snagging a few seminar registrations. Think of your classifieds as a two-step ad. Don't try to sell the seminar in a small classified. Sell them on getting more information.

Trade Publication Ads

If you are doing seminars in a niche market, chances are you'll find at least one or two (maybe more) trade publications you should consider advertising in. Although not as cost effective as email promotion, it usually makes sense to use them to promote your event.

Your promotion efforts in the trade publications will not only generate additional registrants, but you will likely get some in-house seminars and consulting work.

The nice thing about trade publications is that people in that industry usually read them. Most people read them cover to cover. With an effective ad, you **will** be seen.

One of the problems with trade publications is you must plan your seminars well in advance. Depending on the magazine, they may need your ad copy as much as 60 days or more in advance. This isn't as much a problem as it is a hassle. You need to be very organized and book your schedule well in advance.

Magazines are also more effective if you're advertising a series of seminars, not just one. The efficiency of your advertising efforts increases dramatically when you advertise multiple seminars in an ad.

Trade magazines tend to have a fairly long shelf life. Most people keep one magazine on their table or desk at least until the next issue arrives. When the latest issue arrives people save the magazines or cut out the articles and ads that most interests them.

Dollar for dollar trade publications often provide the best return for your marketing dollar outside of email promotions.

If you can also get them to let you write articles for their publications, your ads will be even more effective. Again, there appears to be an implied endorsement.

I suggest you set up your ads in an advertorial style. This makes it look like an article. You may want to test both a three-column and a single-column approach. The more you can make your ad look like editorial copy, the better off you'll be.

Many trade publications will demand that you "slug" your ad. This means that they will slap the word "Advertisement" up at the top of the ad. Don't worry, it rarely depresses response rates.

Radio & TV Advertising

Most advertising on TV and radio for seminars are a waste of time and money. Unless you have extremely deep pockets, promoting using these means are too expensive to test. Since testing must be done before you roll out, the small seminar promoter should avoid both of these means of marketing.

If, on the other hand, you're well financed and have a program that lends itself to a two step promotion, radio and TV may be sensible to try.

The people who have been the most successful with this means of promotion have been the real estate and financial seminar folks. They are normally promoting multiple dates in multiple cities. They are almost always using a two step promotional model. They use radio and TV to fill the rooms and then sell people on a two day weekend event.

Direct Mail

In the not too distant past, direct mail was the primary means of promoting seminars. In the age of the internet, this is changing quickly.

As postage and printing prices rise, it makes sense to find other more cost effective means of marketing your seminar.

I don't suggest that you ignore the use of direct mail, but using my model it will not be your primary means of promoting your events. The problem is the cost associated with printing and postage associated with direct mail.

It is very easy to make money using only email to promote your event. Your fixed costs are virtually nil. The use of direct mail increases your costs and thus your break even number.

Both direct mail and newspaper advertising must have certain elements present in each.

Although I'm doing less and less of it, many people are still using direct mail to promote their events. To make it pay its way, you have to do it right. Earlier in this chapter, I outlined the essential elements of a direct-mail piece or advertising design.

Postcard Mailings

A variation on direct mail that involves long copy sells is the postcard mailing. A postcard mailing is a brief message designed to drive traffic to a Seminar Hot Line or your Web site.

I will often use a postcard mailer when I'm promoting a seminar to my in-house list. This is a group of people who already know and love me. I can use postcards and still get very respectable response to my in-house list.

Whenever I want to redo one of my existing products I'll do a post-card-only mailer to promote the event. I'll limit the attendance to 10 or 12 and then have everyone sit around a boardroom table and record the session.

If I'm promoting a standard event, I'll do a postcard mailing a week before my main direct mail piece. The postcard will promote the upcoming event by giving a Web site address and a seminar hotline number. It will also tell people to be looking for the longer, more in-depth direct mail piece that will follow.

The purpose of the postcard is not to try to sell its recipients on the seminar. That would be absurd. You don't have enough space to make that happen. The purpose of the postcard is to get them to call your seminar hotline or visit your Web site. Let the hotline or the site sell the program for you. If you have an effective hotline, it will, at a minimum, provoke a call from people who want more information. You should be armed with an extensive 8 page fax or email to close the person on registering.

For prospective attendees who live within 250 miles of the seminar location, send a first postcard about five or six weeks before the date of the seminar. Then a week later, send your longer direct mail piece, then a week later, follow up with a different postcard.

If people will have to travel farther than 250 miles, the customer should probably be given a little longer to respond. You may want to add two weeks. Your first postcard would then go out eight weeks before the seminar. Your direct mail piece would go out at six weeks before the date. The last postcard mailer should go out four to five weeks before the date of the seminar.

The key to making your postcards work is the headline. Like any other piece of direct mail, it is vitally important to your success. But, remember your goal is not to get them to agree to sign up for the seminar, but simply to get people to call the hotline or visit the Web site.

Promoting a Bootcamp

How is promoting a bootcamp different from promoting a short seminar? Most of the principles of seminar promotion discussed in the preceding section will work equally well for a bootcamp. But because a bootcamp is by definition longer and generally more expensive than a seminar, your marketing must be more intense and extensive. Since most of your attendees will probably be traveling to the bootcamp site, long lead times become important.

If you're going to use direct mail to promote a bootcamp, you should plan a series of long sales letters starting about 10 to 12 weeks before the event.

As with everything in this area, long copy works best. I suggest you start by sending people a long and detailed sales letter. Then follow up with another fairly long sales letter two weeks later. Follow up with another four-page letter two weeks after that. Then send a final postcard one week after that. This will get as many people as you can get to come.

If you live in a city that people would like to visit during that time of the year, you can host the bootcamp in your home town. If not, consider doing the bootcamp in a location that people **will** perceive as a fun place to be during that time period. Keep in mind that many people will bring their spouse or significant other.

Make it fairly inexpensive for people to bring additional people. Depending on how high a price point you choose, you may want to let spouses or other employees come for no charge or a very nominal additional charge. (Be sure to cover at least the hard, out-of-pocket costs associated with each additional attendee, however.)

I got a solicitation for a bootcamp that I wanted to attend. They charged $1995 for the event, but allowed you to bring up to three additional people from your organization at no additional charge. What did I do? I rounded up three friends and we claimed that we all worked for the same company and we split the total fee. Expect people to do the same at your events. But, who cares? The marginal additional cost of supporting another attendee is minimal.

Web Site Strategies

You must have a web site. I design all of mine as one-page sales letters. The reason I do this is that others who are highly successful do things this way. Using "monkey-see-monkey-do" marketing, I just followed their lead and it has worked quite well. (My partner Dan Shafer over at PublishingProfit.com has some ideas about adding features to this basic concept that we are always experimenting with. Drop by the site for our latest thinking on the subject.)

To collect your free gift (worth $77) send an email to tips@seminarexpert.com

I offer people a low end product (under $50 if possible, but no more than $100). Once they buy, I try to trade them up to higher and higher-priced products and services. People can also sign up to receive marketing tips at no charge. In other words, I try and get them to buy the initial product (called the front-end product) and then convince them to buy one or more of my higher-priced (back-end) products.

Each event you promote should have its own web page to promote that event. I DID NOT say Web site, I said web page. Two very different things. If you're having a bootcamp (like I did) for self publishers, you could put up a page as an extension of an existing site.

The web address might read www.selfpublishingsuccess.com/boot-camp, or possibly bootcamp.selfpublishing.com.This works fine as long as you have a way to track people who come to your site based on referrals from others. Doing this will allow you to make sure that the right people get compensated for registrations.

One common way to do this is with affiliate tracking software such as the program you find at WebMarketingMagic.com. There are other ways of accomplishing this tracking that don't require you to sign up for an affiliate program that are explained in the seminar Dan Shafer presents as a joint venture with me, "Let Technology Give You an Unfair Advantage in Online Marketing."

Regardless of which way you choose to handle it, you need to know when one of your joint venture partners sends someone to your Web site and they sign up for the seminar. Those partners need to feel comfortable that you'll automatically be able to track where referrals come from so they can be confident of being paid for their help.

Make sure you allow people to register for your event on-line. If they came to you through a Web site, they are probably reasonably Web-savvy and will therefore likely expect and appreciate an on-line registration option. It will also take up less of your time to do it this way.

The Web site to promote your event need not include all of the bells and whistles of most Web sites. It should look like a sales letter describing all the features and benefits of attending your event. Resist the temptation to add features that don't have a demonstrable positive impact on your revenue and profits. Particularly avoid graphical and other doodads that increase the time it takes for your site to load into your prospects' and customers' browsers.

Make sure to offer people incentives for signing up immediately. Urgency is even more important on the Web than with direct mail. Once someone clicks away from your site, it's almost impossible to get them to return if they haven't bought something. You should also give them the option to purchase the audio or video tapes of the event.

Why You Shouldn't Use a Speakers Bureau

Speakers bureaus serve as non-exclusive agents for speakers. They generally take somewhere between 20 and 35% of your gross fees. To me this is highway robbery, but they are the going rates.

I don't recommend using speakers bureaus. If you want to learn a lot more about speaking and why I don't think you need to use a speakers bureau, purchase my audio program, "How to Make $3,000 a Day as a Professional Speaker." It will tell you everything you need to know about speakers bureaus and the speaking business in general. You can get more information on the subject at my Web site, www.professionalspeakingsuccess.com.

Marketing the In-House Seminar

Many speakers and seminar leaders will do "in-house" seminars as well as public seminars. Although I'll do them, I don't like them as much as public seminars. Very rarely can you sell anywhere near the amount of product. Many times, companies will buy your product(s) as part of the package you sell them. Even though you can move quite a bit of product, it usually won't be as much as at a public seminar or event.

Just from a fees perspective, however, this is a very profitable side of the seminar business. Expenses are extremely low. Someone sees you doing your thing in a public seminar and they ask you to come do basically the same thing for their employees. Another possible way is that from doing a fair amount of advertising you get a call directly to do an in-house seminar.

Either way produces some very nice, high margin business for you.

I suggest that you schedule in-house seminars on days when you don't have any public seminars scheduled. Use them to fill in your schedule. That's how I've been doing it for years and it's worked well for me.

Some people in this business do exclusively on-site or in-house seminars. If this is more your style, then your marketing methodology will be different. I talk quite a bit about that in my book: *Speaking for Millions.*

Doing a public seminar will generate considerable onsite business. Before they were acquired, this is how CareerTrack used to work. They would give their public seminars as a virtual loss leader. At the end of the seminar they would hand out a form that would give people the opportunity to request someone to call them about an on-site seminar. Sales reps would then follow up on anyone who requested information. Even if they broke even on the public events, they made it back from the onsite events.

During the course of your seminar, drop little hints that you do in-house seminars. When you are delivering your information make sure to weave in stories about work that you've done with other clients who have used you for that purpose.

There are a number of other ways to promote in-house seminars.

First, speak anywhere, anytime you can. Even do it for free if they allow you to sell products. The more you are seen, the greater the chances of someone hiring you for an in-house event. I will frequently pick up in-house seminars and speaking engagements after I speak at a trade show. This is a great showcase for yourself and your talents.

The only time I would do a speech for free is when you're given the opportunity to get in front of precisely the right audience. I might do this myself three or four times a year. Make sure you don't talk yourself into thinking it's the right audience and waste your time.

Second, actively pursue referrals. If you get a chance to speak somewhere, ask them who else might be interested in having you do a seminar for them.

Third, write a book. As an author, you're going to get a lot of calls to speak or do in-house seminars in your area of expertise. (For more information, check out my book, *Publishing for Maximum Profit.*)

Fourth, attend the trade show events in your niche markets. Write articles for their publications. Get to be well-known in your field. This will increase your opportunities for in-house seminar work.

Last, create some good promotional material for yourself. You should have a one-page flyer describing each of the seminar topics you can do in house. Include glowing testimonial letters you get.

Use your evaluations to generate in-house seminars. On the evaluations put a check box for people to check if they want to bring you to their organizations to do a seminar. If you are brought in-house, you'll only make a speaking fee and rarely be able to sell product. This is fine, however, since your cost of marketing is basically zero.

You may also want to prepare a demo video from the tape you have of events that you record.

Do these things and your chances of getting in-house work will be great.

If you want more information, pick up a copy of my book *Speaking for Millions*.

*N*ow That You Have Their Attention
(Marketing 102)

Accepting Credit Cards

Taking credit cards for payment of the seminar registration fee will help to increase the number of people who sign up. If you can't yet accept credit cards, you need to get set up to do so. Card Service International can help. Call them at 1-800-675-6573. They specialize in working with individual entrepreneurs who usually have a hard time getting accepted to receive a merchant account.

I take Visa, MasterCard and American Express. You must take **all** of these. No exceptions. If you can, try to get set up to accept every card. But as a minimum, you must take the top three cards.

You'll need to accept credit cards for registration, product sales, tele-seminars and monthly coaching. One of my clients even pays for consulting by credit card. They do this so that they can get their airline miles. I don't care. I get paid right away when they give me a card. So what if I have to pay 2% to the credit card company? I get my money immediately.

Please, follow my lead.

You should make it as easy as possible for people to give you money. Take checks, credit cards, money orders, cash, whatever people want to give you. I still don't take Discover cards. I should. Make it as easy as is humanly possible for people to open up their wallets and slap some cash into your hand.

If you take checks, will you occasionally get burned? Absolutely. Should this stop you from taking them? Never. It's a cost of doing business.

Getting set up to take credit cards used to require a signed recommendation from the Pope. Things are now slightly easier. Check Appendix A for suggestions on who to talk to about getting set up to take credit cards.

If you're offering a high-priced event, it might also make sense to let people give you their money in installments. Remember, your marginal cost for a seat is pretty low. I only suggest you do this for people who ask. I wouldn't advertise the fact that you do.

I have also begun letting certain people who are skeptical pay me when the event is over. I have **never** been burned using this tactic. If you over-deliver, you'll be in good shape if you go this route on the rare occasion when it's the only way to make a sale.

Toll-Free Number: Just Do It!

The research in this area is conclusive. Providing an 800 number will significantly increase registration numbers, particularly for prospects outside your own area. It also makes you look bigger than you may really be. In most cases, this will help improve your credibility.

I have had the 800 number 1-800-FGLEECK for more than 15 years. Not only is it great to have a vanity 800 number, but there is another marketing value to this number.

Toll-free numbers now include 800, 888, 877, and 866, My having an 800 number is great. It says that I've been around a while. Combine that with the fact that I have a **vanity** 800 number and it says that I've been around a **long** while. My credibility in the marketplace is significantly enhanced by these two facts.

I often highlight these facts in my marketing materials. People may know this intuitively when they see an 800 number, but I like to remind them.

Getting an 800 number is virtually impossible these days. The only way to get an 800 number is to wait for someone to drop their number and you swoop in there and pick one up. How do you do this?

You contact either AT&T, MCI or Sprint and tell a rep that you'll take any 800 number that becomes available. Don't expect to pick up a number that spells anything. It's basically impossible. No one gives up an 800 number that spells anything.

You're still better off with an 800 number that doesn't spell a thing. The credibility factor trumps everything else.

While you're waiting for an 800 number to open up, though, get one of the other toll-free prefix numbers. Most people recognize them as toll-free but anywhere you use it, be sure to label the number "toll-free" to remove all doubt.

Answering the Phones

How Your Phones Are Answered is Important

How your phones are answered will have a significant effect on your profitability. I've seen a number of my clients lose thousands of dollars as a result of poor phone skills.

If you have more than one business, or type of business, operating in your office and only one main incoming phone line, you may need to use a generic phone greeting. This is particularly important if you are dealing with more than one niche market.

My assistant answers the phone, "Good morning/afternoon, Michelle speaking, how can I help you?"

The first thing we want to find out is which seminar they are inquiring about. Asking them directly, however, can have a negative impact on credibility. If they're calling about my self-storage marketing seminar and I ask them if they are calling about that or my catering business seminar or my seminar for speakers, my perceived expertise in their niche gets diminished.

The best way to do this is to ask them which day and month the seminar they are calling about is being held. About 99% of the time, we only offer one seminar on any one day. On the rare occasion that two events are taking place on the same day, we probably end up having to ask people which event they are planning to attend.

When people inquire about a seminar, never immediately say that a seat is available. We ask them which city they are calling about if we are promoting multiple dates. Then we ask them to hold on while we check to determine whether we still have space available. This creates the feeling that a lot of people have been calling and that there is heavy demand.

This is important to create an image of success. No one wants to go to an event attended by very few people. They fear the event will be cancelled. If you follow my advice, that won't be a problem.

The key here is to give people the feeling of scarcity. Making something appear to be in heavy demand gets people to make a decision quicker. It also makes them less likely to quibble about price.

You're also going to want to come up with some sort of an upsell on the phone when they register for the seminar. You might say something like: "Since you're registering before a certain date, we can offer you a special deal on this other item if you buy them as a package."

This is also an opportunity for you to remind them that they can bring a guest for only a small additional fee.

Live Operator vs. Voice Mail

It's always better to have a live person answering your phones. At a minimum, try to have a live operator during business hours.

If you must have an answering machine, make sure that it can handle a large volume of calls. There is nothing more frustrating than calling a business and the machine either doesn't pick up or can't take a message.

If you do have the machine or voice mail system on, make sure that your greeting message is clear and easy to understand.

Setting Up and Using a Hotline

A hotline is a separate line that you set up that gives people a detailed description of what the seminar will cover. It is basically your electronic salesperson that works 24 hours a day, 7 days a week. When people call the line it gives a very detailed pitch of everything that you will cover at the seminar.

It should concentrate on the benefits of attending the seminar. It should have numerical specifics attached to many of the benefits. Something like: "Three things you must do if … " " or "7 deadly mistakes you must avoid when you … "

If you can get away with it, set up the hotline on a residential rather than a commercial (business) line. It's cheaper to set up. I usually get away with residential lines. If you don't advertise them in the yellow pages, your chances of being able to pull this off without alerting the phone company are good.

All you need to do is attach an answering machine or a voice mail system that will give you the ability to create a long outgoing message. Remember, the hotline message can never be too long, only too boring.

People at my seminars who hear me talk about this hotline will frequently say to me, "I would never listen to a 10-minute message about a seminar, blah, blah, blah." My answer is simple. I don't care what **you** think, I care about what your **prospective attendees** think or do. They're the ones we are trying to reach. If people are seriously interested in attending an event they will listen to a message that goes on for 10 or more minutes. Why? Because they are interested. They haven't heard about it before.

Remember this. If people are going to pay a lot of money, they need to be "sold" to a certain extent. Also, different people respond to different approaches. Some people will respond to the written approach. Others will respond to a verbal "pitch."

Prepare a script and read it into the machine. Ask some people to listen to the hotline message. Get their feedback. Make suggested changes that you think make sense.

People usually respond positively because they are hearing the voice of the person who will be doing the seminar. Don't use a professional voice person to do this. The person who does the seminar must record the hotline message as well.

If you use postcards to promote your event, it is wise to send people to your hotline. There isn't much selling space available on a postcard, so you need to concentrate on sending them to the hotline.

Additionally, I put the hotline message number on any and all advertising.

Appendix A has a sample hotline message for one of my seminars that you can use as a model for creating your own.

Getting Them to Sign Up

Have a System

At a recent trade show I attended as a speaker, I witnessed a nightmare. The keynote speaker was due to speak at 9 a.m. People who were attempting to register before the speech encountered huge lines and an extremely inefficient registration process. Many of the people missed more than half of the keynoter's speech. What a mess!

Admittedly, some of the people were trying to register at 8:58 a.m. and expecting to get in to see the speaker's entire presentation. Most of them, however, had come well in advance. The fault clearly lay with the seminar promoter.

Don't let the same thing happen to you.

When people show up to attend your seminar/workshop you must have a system for processing them efficiently. This system must take care of two things, payments and packets.

First, you need to make sure that payment is handled. Second, you need a way to make sure they get their packets of information. Third, you'll want to make sure they sign something indicating they picked up their packets. Asking people to initial or quickly sign next to their names will assure that no one gets two sets of your potentially expensive materials. Also, you'll occasionally have a sly operator who will slip in and give a common name like Bob Smith and try and pick up materials to steal them.

To help make this happen you need one alphabetized list (a roster) of everyone registered for the event. This list should show whether and how people have paid their fee. That same sheet can also be used as a "pick-up" sheet. Ask them to sign next to their name to indicate they picked up their packet of materials.

You should have each of the packets pre-prepared with everything including name badges, meal tickets, handouts, promotional material, etc.

Some people like to create participant name tags at the time of registration. The reason is the frequent misspelling of peoples' names. This is a great concept, but it can dramatically slow down the registration process. If you carefully take their names down at the time of registration, you'll only need to correct a few misspelled names. This is a lot more efficient than doing each one on site.

Those who haven't paid should be sent to a separate line to take care of the payment process. Don't let these folks hold up the rest of the group who are just picking up their materials for the event.

People who paid by credit card should have their credit card receipts in their packets. Be careful **not** to screw this one up. People hate the idea of someone else seeing their credit card numbers. If they get someone else's credit card receipt, they know that someone else is running around with theirs.

If they paid by check, include some other kind of receipt. Even though I use my checks as my receipts, some people still want a separate receipt. Prepare one for them. It doesn't have to be elaborate, but it should be included.

For those who pay at the event itself, you should make three forms of payment available.

Credit cards will account for the majority of your seminar registrations. For most people who do seminars credit cards represent more than 70% of their payments. You have two options. Either you can bring a credit card machine and process on-site or you can call them in immediately after people register.

It's preferable to have a machine attached to a phone line so that you can do both immediately. This way you can generate a receipt and find out if a credit card is valid. If you can't process at the time of registration (and I don't do this at all my events, either), then make sure to process the charges immediately after registration. Try to do it before the first break if your numbers will allow it. Certainly get it done before the lunch break.

There are, of course, lots of reasons for a person's credit card transaction not to go through. These run the gamut from errors on the card processing service's end to theft and fraud. The person at your seminar may not know that his or her spouse just went on a shopping spree with that card. So if a credit card is refused (and you've tried to run it through at least twice, preferably three times), you should approach the individual discreetly and ask if they have another card since that one was declined. Be sure to do this early enough in the seminar so that you can be assured of being paid before they end up getting the seminar free.

Checks are a little tougher. I haven't yet gone to a system which guarantees checks that I receive. I'm not even sure how such a system might work or if such systems exist for those of us who aren't running cash-register operations. As I said earlier, if you take checks, you'll occasionally get burned. It's part of the cost of doing business. But if the amount of the check is sufficient, it's probably worth hiring a collection bureau or, in some states at least, filing a criminal fraud complaint against the perpetrator.

Some people will want to pay by cash. **Make sure you set up so they can**. Always accept cash. Have a system for how it is handled. I usually want only my own people to handle the cash registrations. I would not delegate this to a temp or someone that I didn't know that well. Figure out from the price of your seminar what kind of change you're likely to need and have plenty of it on hand.

If you are doing a small group (25 or fewer), you can handle all this processing yourself with a minimum of problems. Make sure you have a good list of all the pre-registered attendees. Also make sure that next to the name you have an indication of whether or not they are paid and by what means.

I like the idea of having a registration table out in front of the room where you are holding the event. Make sure that you have name tags laid out in alphabetical order on the table. This way people can quickly and easily find their name badges and/or materials for the seminar.

Organize yourself properly and your life will be much easier. Follow my example or create a system of your own. Whichever way you go, have a **system**.

Online Registration

Assuming you have a Web site set up (you do, don't you?), it also makes sense for you to allow people to register online as well.

If you have others remarketing your seminar, you can set up an affiliate program to automatically track who sent you the referral.

All of this can be done using tools like Web Marketing Magic at www.webmarketingmagic.com.

Providing people with the option to register online is in keeping with the key principle of making it as easy as possible for people to give you their money.

Use Early Enrollment Incentives

You must give people some incentive to call **immediately** when they find out about your seminar. In the first seminar I offered on consulting, I gave people $10 off if they registered before the day of the seminar. This helped get people to sign up immediately.

Many seminar providers will give people a step stair discount based on how quickly they sign up. For example, a $225 seminar scheduled for March 28 might start out costing $175 before March 1, $195 before March 21, and the full $225 thereafter.

This will help to smooth out the demand curve. It will make the registrations come in at a more even pace. This will help reduce the drastic "heart attack curve." You will get your registrations at a much more even pace.

Again, test this one.

My latest is to give the first 10 people who sign up a video worth $99. This seems to work, but it can be expensive.

The best incentive I've found is a critique coupon. This is a small piece of paper that I value at $150. It allows people to send me any piece of promotional literature for a critique. This has a very high perceived value to the potential seminar attendee and low cost to you. (Incidentally, I've found that most people don't take advantage of these things anyway.)

This is the key to any incentive that you offer a potential seminar attendee. Think for yourself about coming up with something that is inexpensive, yet has high perceived value. This is what you will want to offer potential seminar attendees.

Giving Them "Comfort Information"

After people register, you need to get them a packet of information. This way they feel like they are getting something for their money. In addition to a "welcome" letter, this packet should include an agenda. This will give people a rough idea of the time frame for both speakers and breaks. If you're running a high-priced bootcamp, you might even send out this information in advance of the event. At least have it on the registration table or in their registration packets.

You should also include bios of all of the speakers who will be presenting. You can also add to the packet by including information about the seminar locale and any special events that may be going on during the days of the seminar. You can usually get this information from the hotel or the local convention and visitors' bureau.

If you're holding an event where there will be a lot of speakers, I also like to include some evaluation forms in this initial packet. Not only will this make things easier, it will also show that you're serious about getting feedback.

Some Frequently Asked Questions About Registration

When people call to register on the phone, you usually only have one shot at them. You cannot have morons handling your registration line(s). It will cost you money.

Whomever answers the phone must be knowledgeable about the event, courteous and sales-oriented. Remember, the goal of receiving that call is to get a credit card number and make the caller feel good and comfortable giving it to you.

Whoever answers the phone must make people feel like spaces still remain for the event but that they are going fast. There must be urgency created to make people register **now**.

Many people will want to know how many people are registered. There are usually three reasons for this question. First, they are your competition. They are checking out how you're doing. Second, many people have signed up for an event only to have it cancelled. They've been screwed making plane and hotel reservations and have a legitimate concern. Finally, they are just curious as to how many of the people will show up. I know I always am.

The correct way to handle this question is to say that you're really not sure. Tell them that registrations are being collected from a number of different sources and only your boss has all of the numbers. Assure them that you don't cancel events and then get their credit card numbers.

Using this approach will only disappoint your competition. They will find out after your event anyway. Someone will tell them. It always works that way.

Remember that in the seminar registration business people tend to register at fairly predictable times. If people have to travel and book hotel rooms, you'll get most of your registrations well before the event itself. In my case, less than 20% of the registrations for our bootcamps come in the last 14 days before the event.

This is **not** the case with one day seminars held in cities where people don't have to travel overnight. In this case, **most** of the registrations come in the last 14 days before the event. To prevent this heart attack seminar registration curve, give people plenty of incentive to register early.

$\mathcal{S}$ educing the Undecided
(Guerrilla Marketing Tactics)

At several points in this book, I've mentioned the "Heart Attack" Seminar Registration Curve. In this chapter, I'm going to focus exclusively on that issue and some techniques for avoiding it. You've heard some of these ideas before in different contexts, but they're worth repeating and emphasizing. Trust me.

The "Heart Attack" Seminar Registration Curve

People who have never done seminars before often experience an incredible amount of anxiety and stress. The major stress relates to the rate at which the registrations come in. They come in slowly at first and then dramatically pick up within two weeks or less of the seminar date, depending on the length and location of the event.

I call it the "Heart Attack" curve because the novice seminar promoter often freaks out waiting for the registrations to come in. Sometimes you get as much as 50% or more in the last several days before the date of the seminar.

Events like bootcamps that require travel and hotel reservations generally fill up sooner than shorter events. I also like the idea of promoting to people in the last two weeks or so and sending them to a site called www.site59.com. This site allows people to make last-minute travel and hotel arrangements at discounted prices. Using this system may encourage some people to come at the last minute.

Using Bonuses to Seduce More Buyers

I also like to load a lot of bonuses into the seminar seduction routine. I will give people all kinds of bonuses for registering before a specific date. These would include things like consulting time with me over the phone, free special reports, an eBook or two and a discount coupon to attend other seminars and events.

I try to make these bonuses **very** appealing. I also try to make most of them digitally deliverable so I have virtually no cost but my time. Even when I offer people 30 minutes of my time over the phone as a bonus, only one in 20 will take me up on it. Sad, but true. Consulting time on the phone has a very high perception of value, but a very low use rate. What a great bonus.

Bonuses are something you must make sure you deliver on. I have never done a seminar where someone hasn't mentioned something to me about the bonuses they receive for attending. Don't forget to make good on your promises.

I sometime like to send them separately and a few days apart. This way people think they have gotten even more value than they really have.

Offer One-on-One Consultations as a Premium

Another very effective way to get people to sign up for your events is to offer them consulting time before, during or after the event.

It makes for a long day, but it can dramatically increase enrollment. People get to sit at the feet of the master (you) one-on-one for 20-30 minutes to get their individual questions answered. I would only recommend you do this in conjunction with a high priced event or seminar. Why give away your time unless you have to? For many people this will be what gets them to register.

Try to get these consultations scheduled before the event. If you have more demand than you can accommodate on-site before the seminar, arrange to give them the same amount of time (or slightly more) over the phone in the days leading up to the event.

Putting Customers on a Hot Seat They'll Love!

Hot seats are a great concept that you should definitely use when appropriate. Here's how they work. You set aside time, usually towards the end of the session (or day), to bring a certain number of people up in front of the group. I usually have each person come up for about 10 minutes.

You ask them to briefly introduce themselves. Then you ask them to share with the group their biggest problem that relates to the topic of the seminar. Hopefully they share a business and not a personal problem! You (along with the other "experts" if you're doing a bootcamp) then give them your best suggestions. Allow other audience members, for a short time, to offer their suggestions. Jump in if they get too far off track.

This works extremely well because it allows you to answer specific questions from individual members of the group. It significantly increases the value of your event. It is as close as you can get to giving people individual assistance during the seminar itself.

The beauty of the hot seat concept is that it isn't just the people **on** the hot seat who benefit. Many of the questions raised and answered will be helpful to other members of the group.

Whenever I do an event of two or more days, I always make the hot seats a bonus. I restrict the reservation of the hot seats to the first 20 people who would like to do them.

If I myself were attending an event where they had hot seats I would sign up immediately to make sure I got to be on the hot seat. Not everyone feels the same way. Many of your attendees are deathly afraid of getting up in front of the group and baring their souls.

There are, however, many people who feel like I do. For them, the opportunity to be on the hot seat will encourage them to register early. It always has that effect on me!

Offer the hot seats to the first X number of people who sign up and want them. When you run out, tell people that you'll put them on a waiting list for a hot seat. Make sure they understand that you aren't guaranteeing that they will get one. They only get their chance if someone doesn't show up or a participant decides not to do theirs.

Outside-the-Box Promotional Ideas

Discounting in Return for Help at Your Event

When I do my own large seminars I generally try to recruit a few volunteers to help me. The best way I've found to get people to help you out is to offer a few individuals a reduced rate or free admission to your event. Don't do this too early in the sales cycle.

If you're promoting a seminar for March, don't start making this option available until the middle of February. You obviously want to capture all of your paying customers first. Those people who may have wanted to come to the event but couldn't afford it are the people who may come as volunteers.

The most important thing to remember is that you need people who can and will really help. To make sure that this happens, you may want to put together a very simple one-page agreement. This agreement would enumerate their responsibilities in exchange for free or reduced-rate admission to your event.

Also, be sure to tell your volunteers that they can't let anyone know that they're attending for free or a reduced rate.

I've been extremely lucky when I've used volunteers this way. Most of the time I get people who are highly competent and more than willing to help. I think it might have something to do with the quality of events that I offer. People who know they are getting to attend a great event for less than full price usually give you their best efforts.

Sponsorships by Associations or Organizations

One of the best ways to do seminars is to get a trade association to sponsor your event. Using this technique, you can reduce up-front costs and risk virtually nothing. In most cases, the association or sponsoring organization will give you a split of the revenue that comes in. You'll want to set up some kind of a minimum guarantee for the event.

A relationship like this can take many different forms.

The key to doing this right is to create a partnership with the organization. If at the end of the event, you make all of the money, they will not use you again. Find a formula that is fair for both of you.

Paying Others to Promote Your Seminar

Some seminar promoters will hire people to help promote their events. If you do this, I suggest you put them on a straight commission basis. Paying people this way makes a lot of sense. Paying anyone on a straight salary inevitably doesn't work. Don't do it. If people will work for you on straight commission, hire as many of them as you possibly can. After all, what's the downside?

One-Shot vs. Double-/Triple-Shot Mailings

A one-shot promotion is when you send prospects a single promotional mailing to get them to attend your event. If you are doing a traditional mailing it is more likely that you would use this approach given that the total cost of the mailings increases each time you mail. With an in-house email list there is no additional cost to mail more than once. In that case you would do a sequenced campaign consisting of two or three mailings.

If you're doing direct mail, you mail to them two or three times. In many cases, your second and third mailers will continue to be profitable, just not **as** profitable as your first mailer.

To use this technique effectively, you need to know the average value of a seminar attendee. In my case, seminar attendees in some of my niche markets are worth an average of more than $400 per person. This amount is determined by averaging the total amount of money attendees will spend with you over a lifetime (i.e., before they stop buying entirely or have purchased all your products).

If you're charging $197 for a seminar, it may make sense to continue to acquire customers at $200 a piece knowing that you'll make an additional $200 from them over their lifetime of association with you.

If you're just starting out in the seminar business, I would recommend against your doing multiple mailings until you have a good idea of your costs and an approximate idea of lifetime customer value. In other words, here's your favorite word again: **test**.

Free 90-Minute Sales Pitch

Many higher-priced seminars are promoted via a free 90-minute presentation that is really an information-packed sales pitch. You will generally refer to these as "free information seminars." If you're a good salesperson for your events, this can be a very effective means of promoting a relatively expensive, lengthier event.

This technique works best in more general-interest seminars. It would be difficult to use this technique when promoting to a small niche market. The opportunities just aren't there.

A "just show up" Registration Model

Seminars will sometimes be advertised and not permit people to register in advance. This is a very interesting approach and one I have used myself on occasion. Here is how the thinking goes. If you are spending money on advertising and promotion, you aren't going to cancel your event no matter how few people show up. You've sunk all of your costs and you'll be looking to recover some money no matter how poorly registration goes.

Given this fact, you tell people in your ad that there will be NO pre-registration. People must register an hour before the event and only the first "X" amount of people will be allowed in. People reading this ad will be intrigued by someone who advertises this way. They know that the event will not be cancelled because of the way you have structured registration.

Your prospective participants will perceive you as pretty cocky. This may work to your advantage depending on the type of people you're trying to attract.

The only downside is not knowing what your exact count will be. This will make it tough to judge how big a meeting room to reserve. You'll learn your numbers through testing. When you're just starting out and using this system, always get a slightly smaller, rather than slightly larger, meeting room than you think you'll need.

It is much better to have to turn people away than to present to an empty room.

*O*n Site: Getting Ready to Deliver the Goods

Introduction

Now that you've got people coming to your event, you've got to delight them with the seminar itself. You need to do this for a few reasons.

First, you don't want them to ask for their money back. Second, you want them to buy a lot of product from you. Third, you want them to come back to future events. Finally, you want them to buy your consulting services.

If you blow it at the seminar itself, you'll lose on all four of these points.

When people come to your events, they expect a minimum of two things. First, they want someone who is a good presenter. Second, they want someone who will give them lots of usable and relevant content. These two are equally important; one without the other is a failure. If you're weak in either of these areas, get some help. If you need a referral in either the content or presentation skill area, contact us.

Being good is not enough; you must be **great**!

Many seminar promoters do only the minimum to fulfill their contractual obligations to their attendees and customers. I suggest you significantly exceed the expectations of your audience. Do more than they expect. Doing things this way will increase product sales and increase your enrollment at future events.

Giving you a complete list of specific things that go into making a great seminar and presentation would occupy another book this size. The best advice I can give you in a small space is to concentrate on those things you can do that impress the heck out of people but cost you very little "out-of-pocket" dollars.

The rest of this chapter offers some things to keep in mind when you present your seminar to make sure you do it right!

Your Look

I have a trademark speaking wardrobe. I always wear my famous Coogi sweaters when I present. These are these very bright and colorful sweaters that I got turned on to in Australia. These work best for me. They fit my personality and my results are always good when I'm wearing them.

Find out what works for you. Note what you're wearing each time you present and tabulate the results. See what you tend to sell best in. Whatever works best, wear that outfit all the time.

You may find that your most effective wardrobe varies with your target audience. Some kinds of attendees may respond better to a suit-and-tie look while others will buy like mad when you wear jeans and a humorous T-shirt. Within the bounds of good taste, you should experiment and keep track.

Once you find something that works well, don't mess with success.

Psych Yourself Up

When you are giving a seminar, you are "on stage" for a good part of the day. As you know if you've done any seminars (and as you'll soon find out if you haven't), there is a combination of exhilaration and exhaustion that occurs in conjunction with such performance. To be at your best, you probably need to "psych yourself up" to get into performance and selling mode before you start your seminar.

There are many ways of doing this. Only you can figure out what works for you. Some people use affirmations, others use meditation, still others use physical exercise. Whatever you use, make sure and put yourself into the right mental state before you start or your products sales will suffer.

Be Physically Fit

Giving a seminar is hard work. It can be fun and exhilarating, but there's no doubt it is physically draining. It's important that you come into your seminar room in as good physical condition as you can get. This doesn't mean you have to be some kind of fitness nut or spend hours every day working out in a gym. (If you're inclined to do those things, of course, they won't **hurt** you!)

The night before your seminar, you should consider following a few simple rules that many seminar leaders have discovered over the decades this business has existed.

- First, eat a light but satisfying dinner, as early as you can. Many seminar leaders report that avoiding red meat the night before a presentation helps them feel more energy in the morning. You might experiment with that. Note that this might require you to arrive in your seminar city a day early rather than simply the night before, so that you can get a meal before too late at night, local time.

- Second, get a normal amount of sleep the night before the seminar. It's important to be well-rested, but if you, for example, arrive at your site city exhausted and then sleep two or three hours longer than you are accustomed to sleeping, you might find that works against you.

- Third, avoid sugary or starchy breakfast foods. Fruit plates, egg-and-meat plates (in moderation) or grain and cereal-based foods are a better regimen than donuts, pastries, and waffles.

- Finally, if you are traveling to present your seminar, call your significant other before you go to the seminar room, assuming time zones allow that. This will both provide you encouragement and remove or reduce the likelihood that you'll be dwelling on home concerns when you should be focusing on the room and your attendees.

- Another technique that helps me greatly in dealing with the stress of staging an event — or even just being in this business! — is meditation. It's definitely worth you experimenting with it to see how it works for you.

Get to Your Room Early

Things can and do go wrong. You must get to the room where you're doing your event at least an hour ahead of your scheduled start time, two hours early in the case of a larger or longer event. If you're handling registration yourself, you should be there an hour before registration is set to open. If you're at a hotel and your program starts first thing in the morning, see if you can get in to see the room the night before.

Why are you there that early? For a number of important reasons.

First, you have to check all of the audio and/or video systems you'll be using. If it's a crucially important event it's important that you have back-ups for all of your systems. If are selling video tapes for example, you'll need to have a backup video recorder. If you're selling the audio tapes you'll need a back up audio recording device.

If you're using any visual aids or computer equipment, check the hardware you'll be using to make sure it's working and how to make things happen.

You'll also want to get a "feel" for the room. Walk around the room. Check the microphone to find out where the "hot spots" are. Hot spots are those places where your microphone will give you a ton of feedback when you walk under them. Walk up the stairs of the stage or risers. Get a feel for the space that you'll be in soon.

Water is important. Make sure there's a pitcher of water at or near the podium. I like to have the water at slightly cooler than room temperature. I also like to squeeze a few lemons into the water before I start. Experts tell us that ice water is very bad for your voice, so avoid using it during the seminar. You'll undoubtedly find a water system that works for you.

Check Room Setup and Seating Arrangements

Seating Arrangement Options

There are a few standard seating arrangements that you can use at your events. These include theatre style (where you have chairs with nothing in front of them), classroom style, U-shape, and round tables.

If you have an event that lasts longer than a few hours, don't use theatre style seating. Although you can pack a lot more people into a smaller room, it's difficult for people to tolerate sitting that way for any length of time. People need a place to write.

A U-shape (also known as a horseshoe) is best used with groups under 25. This is where you set up tables in the shape of a U. You then deliver your presentation within the U itself. This is best to use if you want to set up classroom style but you don't have a large crowd.

For groups of more than 25 where there will be a lot of writing and note taking you'll want to set up classroom style This is where every participant has a table in front of them.

Round tables are a favorite of many presenters where there will be a lot of group exercises. I like using round tables for seminars where there is a lot of interactivity among participants.

People have to be seated comfortably to increase the chances of their buying. The more comfortable you can make them without making them sleepy the better off you'll be. For presentations longer than two hours, never seat people theatre style.

Scoping Out the Room

The people who set up the seminar meeting room for you may not get it exactly right. It's important to check the room setup and the seating arrangement before it's too late to fix them.

Make sure that you and your visual screens (if you're using them) can be seen from all the seats. Take note of where the projector is located and sit in the seats whose views might be obscured by it. If those seats don't work well, relocate the chairs or have the hotel staff do so.

Where do you control the room temperature and lighting? Do you understand how to use them? If not, get someone to show you. Few things are more disruptive to a smooth-flowing seminar than to have these kinds of logistical issues get in the way.

Is there enough space between chairs, both side to side and front to back? Are your attendees going to be comfortable sitting for several hours? You can't always control this, but if you start early enough, you often can.

Is all the equipment you need in place? Easel? Markers? White board? Eraser? Overhead projector? If you're using any projection equipment, do you have at least one spare bulb for each unit?

If you've asked for a classroom setup where everyone is seated at a table, do you have pens or pencils (maybe with your company's advertising on them?) in place? Are there writing tablets for everyone, assuming they're not included in the seminar packet you're going to pass out? Sometimes in classroom settings, it's a good idea to have water and perhaps some hard candies available around the room as well.

Use a Wireless Remote Microphone

I own my own microphones. Both of them are cordless. I've got both a hand-held and a lavaliere mike. If you do a lot of seminars, it's a good idea to own your own mikes. This gives you control over your most important instrument as a speaker.

I prefer the cordless mikes because of the freedom of movement they allow. The only downside to a cordless mike is the occasional interference you'll pick up. You can eliminate most of this by getting a "true diversity" mike.

Hand-held mikes are the way to go in my opinion. Although a lavaliere mike will make it easier for you to work an overhead at the same time, a hand-held gives you the ability to create a lot more vocal variety. How many singers have you seen that used anything other than a hand-held mike? The reason for this is that they can move the mike closer or further away from their mouths for effect.

The only singers you'll see these days who use those space age looking headsets are those who do a lot of jumping around as part of their act.

Go with a hand held, remote mike!

Meet and Greet Your Attendees Before the Event

Meet and greet your audience members if possible before the event starts. I've done it both ways and the numbers always seem to be better when I get to press the flesh before I start.

Checklist to Bring to Engagements and Events

Carry a checklist of everything related to your product sales process. If you have the checklist you'll never forget a crucial item. With one less thing to worry about, your product sales will improve.

From the Podium: Delivering the Seminar Goods

Enough getting ready, already! Let's dive into the things you need to do to make your seminar so great you'll have people signing up for your next one before this one's even over!

Starting the Seminar Right

The way you start your seminar is vitally important. How you start and how you end are crucial to how your event will be perceived.

I would open a keynote speech with a story, but with seminars I like to open with introductions. Remember, the primary intent of a speech is to motivate and secondarily to educate. Seminars are just the opposite. That being the case, starting with introductions makes sense.

Start and End on Time, But Control What That Means

You must always start and end on time. There are no exceptions to this rule.

I make it very clear in all of my promotional literature that we start and end exactly on time. I also put this on the confirmation I send to people. Additionally, we remind people of this fact when they register. I start **on time**. People will respect you for doing this, even those who come late.

If you can't do it any other way, leave out levels of detail that are less important than main points. This means that you must mark information that you can leave out. This way, if you see you are running short on time, you know what can be left out as you go.

Never penalize people who made it to your event on time by starting late, Reinforce the behavior by being prompt. If you have a multi-day event, people will get the message and get into their seats on time the following day, particularly if you deliver good information.

Many people make plans for what they will do after your event is over. They make these plans based on the time frames you give them. Stick to them. Many people don't want to miss any of your seminar, but neither do they want to miss meeting a friend for dinner.

If you list the topics to be covered at your seminar never put exact times those items will be covered. Put the items in the order they will be covered and divide them into a morning and afternoon line up.

If you decide to ignore this advice and provide exact start times for subjects, I guarantee you that some anal-retentive type will look at his or her watch and say: "It's 10:30, why aren't we covering thus and so?" This is deadly. Don't lock yourself into a time frame.

Things happen during the course of the seminar which may cause you to spend more or less time covering certain topics. Even if you have done the seminar 50 times before, this may still happen. A given group may need more or less concentration on a given issue. Keep yourself flexible.

To Introduce or Not to Introduce?

If your group is small enough and you have enough time, it is always a good idea to let people introduce themselves. This not only helps you as a facilitator, it also allows the participants to "show off" to the rest of the group. Additionally, it improves the quality of networking at the breaks.

As a seminar leader, your biggest problem with introductions will be people exceeding the time you've given them. You prevent this by defining what you expect before you start going around the room. At that point it's also wise to tell people what you'll do if they exceed the time frame you give them. This way, if you have to cut them short, they won't be offended.

If you do have to exercise this prerogative, do it in a fun and entertaining manner. Try not to be harsh.

Regardless of how long an event you're having, it just isn't practical to let people introduce themselves if the group size is over 100 people. That might not hold true if you had a five-day event. Events of that length would generally afford you the time to let people introduce themselves even if you had 200 or more people.

Even with a group of 100 people and a half day seminar, you could let everyone stand up and quickly tell the group their name and field of specialization or occupation.

With groups of less than 30 people, and at least a two-hour event, I will normally ask people to give the group their name, their field or occupation, and one specific reason why they came to the event.

While people are introducing themselves, take notes. This will allow you to customize your message. With a small group, I like to keep a little seating chart where I put peoples' names and take notes about them.

After you go around the room, you need to introduce yourself. This is an important step to establish credibility.

The first few minutes you spend in front of a group are crucial. This is where you establish the relationship people will not forget. Your goal is to get people to both like and respect you. It is also to set the stage for making sure that you sell a boatload of product.

A Great Index Card Idea

Here's a creative seminar idea I've seen used very effectively. At the beginning of your event, ask everyone to write down on an index card you supply, the question they would most like to get answered at your event.

Now, ask them to stand up when their question is answered. Have them tell the group what the question was, how it was answered and then have them tear the card in pieces and fling those pieces in the air.

This exercise does two things.

First, it creates a very celebratory environment.

Second, it reinforces the information by having someone get up and repeating it.

Before the end of the event go around and collect the cards that haven't yet been torn up. Bring them up to the front. Read the questions out loud. Answer them completely. Ask the individual who wrote the question whether you've answered the question to their satisfaction. If they say yes, tear it up and throw it in the air.

The Action Idea Sheet

At the beginning of the seminar I often ask the attendees to pull out a sheet of paper (or in some cases I have them preprinted) and put the words "Action Ideas" at the top. I ask them to write down the really great ideas they hear during the seminar whenever they come up.

It's a good idea, too, to guarantee them that they'll get at least three (or five, or some other number) action ideas during the course of the seminar. Then, at the close of the seminar, go around the room and have a few people tell the group how many action ideas they got. If you give a good seminar, people will get two or three times as many action ideas as you guarantee.

I review the sheet after coming back from every break. I so exceed peoples' expectations that they will buy more product because they'll assume that I do the same things with the products I'm offering. Don't let them down or your returns will be high.

Importance of Visual Aids

Speakers and seminar leaders who spend huge amounts of time worrying about their visual aids are misguided. I've seen lots of presenters with all kinds of fancy PowerPoint presentations, but who were only average presenters. Your visual aids should complement your "performance"; they should never **be** the performance.

I see a lot of presenters who use their visual aids as a means of masking a very average presentation. I'm usually suspicious of people with a really razzle-dazzle visual presentation. If you have a great presentation you frankly don't need a stunning visual presentation. This isn't to say that you can't do both.

In my opinion you should be your own best visual aid. You've got to learn how to move on stage and capture peoples' attention.

If your visual presentation adds to your presentation, then by all means use it. Just don't rely on it and make it the centerpiece of your presentation.

Without seeing your presentation it is really difficult to give you very general guidelines. The one criticism I can give you of most of the visuals that I see used at presentations has to do with the amount of information that people try and pack onto one slide or overhead.

Here are some additional hints if you are going to use visuals effectively:

Remember the 6x6 Rule

Be economical with the text on your visuals. Stick to a maximum of six words per line and a maximum of six lines. The visuals you present don't have to be a verbatim transcript of what you'll be telling people. (In fact, one of the most annoying things you've probably experienced yourself is attending a seminar where the speaker simply reads his or her slides.)

Instead, think of your visuals as an executive summary of the information you want to present.

Keep Quantity of Visuals Reasonable

I've been at seminars where a person went through 50 slides in a 60 minute presentation. This is absurd. I can't give you an exact number, but keep them limited to your essential information that needs to be highlighted. If you want to give people all kinds of specific information, do it in the form of a handout.

Keep Things Simple

The simpler you can make things in your verbal presentation, the better. The same thing holds true for any visuals that you use. Give your visuals the old 4th grader test. If you show them to a 10 year old kid and they can understand them, you're on the right track. Take the complex and make it simple. People will appreciate this approach.

Have Someone Else Proofread Everything

There is nothing more embarrassing than having typos or factual errors on your visuals. No matter how many times you go over the material yourself, you won't be able to catch your own mistakes. Have at least one, if not two or three people proofread your visuals for typos and factual accuracy.

Use Technology Where Appropriate
(But Have Low-Tech Backup)

It's perfectly acceptable to use a razzle-dazzle video presentation if that's the industry you're in or the group you're appealing to. Use it where it makes sense. Don't just use the flashy approach to show people that you can. Appropriateness is the key word. There are times when the old flip chart makes the most sense. Don't be afraid to use this and other low-tech devices if they make sense.

I can't tell you how many times I've seen a video projector go down during a seminar. The problem is that many presenters **only** have their presentations on the computer. Don't be one of them. Make sure that you carry some standard overheads as a back up just in case. (In fact, to be triply sure, carry a hard copy of your presentation and the associated notes. For most presentations, you should be able to deliver the material nearly as effectively even if power goes out.)

Have Some Fun

Unless you're a humorist, you don't want to try to make people cackle with laughter with every visual you put up, but you do want to lighten things up a bit every so often. Even the stodgiest group of corporate types will appreciate the occasional visual that tries to make things a little less serious. I tend to be somewhat less than politically correct in my humor. I don't necessarily recommend that you follow my lead, but that's my style.

Keeping Their Attention

All the great material in the world presented with perfect and appropriate visual aids won't help your audience if they're asleep or distracted. You have an obligation to keep your attendees alive, alert, awake, and enthusiastic.

Stimulate All Their Senses

Different people learn best in different ways. Some people learn best through reading the printed word. Others prefer to learn by listening. Still others want to watch a visual presentation.

During your presentation, you also need to stimulate as many of your participants' senses (sight, smell, taste, touch, and hearing) to be most effective.

As you design the content for your seminar, try to find a way to stimulate all of these senses. Don't try to force it. If it makes sense to use them, fine. If not, don't work too hard to find a way to work each one in. Keep in mind, though, that the more of them you can stimulate, the more likely you are to teach something to everyone in your audience.

People Love Lists

Whether it's the "7 Habits of Highly Successful People" or "101 Ways to Keep Your Man Happy," people love lists.

People find it easy to learn when you give them a very specific number of things that they either should or shouldn't do. I can't tell you with certainty why this is the case, but I suspect it's because people like being given a very specific set of instructions on what to do or what **not** to do.

Give people lists of dos and don'ts , steps to take, items to memorize, and key summary points where appropriate in your presentations.

Storytelling Secrets

Great stories can significantly improve your seminars. Many people are born story-tellers. Others can learn to tell them effectively. Unlike jokes (which there are some people who decidedly can **not** learn to tell), everyone can learn to tell a story well enough to be interesting.

There are a few points to remember when you tell stories.

Never invent stories or steal them from other speakers and claim them as your own. Not only is it unethical, but the story won't flow like it's truly yours. Why? Because it's not! There are plenty of real-life experiences that you can share that will turn into great "signature" stories after you perfect them.

Keep a story file. Every time something interesting, instructive or amusing happens to you, write it down. Put your stories into a story file by category on your computer. When you put your seminar modules together, look through these files and see which ones fit.

If you don't write down a story, you'll probably forget it pretty quickly, so protect yourself by putting everything down on paper.

To be effective, unless you're a natural, practice telling the story repeatedly. It is seldom that a great story emerges when told for the first time. It takes time to perfect them.

If you want to be funny, tell stories, not jokes. If you tell a joke and it flops, everyone will know it. If you tell a story that you think is funny and nobody laughs, it's just a story. No one will know that you intended it to be funny.

Remember that different people are funny to different degrees. Don't try to be funnier than you are.

Stories aren't just told to amuse. They are told to instruct and illuminate. Don't feel that every story you tell has got to have your seminar attendees rolling in the aisles. (If this happens, however, you would probably have a great career as a humorist or after-dinner speaker.)

To collect your free gift (worth $77) send an email to tips@seminarexpert.com

Get People Moving

Sitting in seminars and workshops can get tiring. Find ways to get people up and moving around during your events, but do so with a purpose.

One way to do this is to ask your group a multiple-choice question with 4 possible answers. Ask people to answer the question by going to a particular corner of the room. This gets people up and moving around, but with a very specific purpose.

Please don't let me catch you doing any of those tired and ridiculous exercises where you ask people to get up and give their neighbor a neck massage. Not only is this exercise overdone, it's **stupid**! Some people don't like strangers touching them and it doesn't prove a point.

Another physical exercise that works very well to both give you information and get people up and moving around is this technique.

You ask your audience members questions. If the answer is true they stand up. If false, they stay seated. You can get a survey of your audience as well as give them some physical activity using this effective technique.

Breaking People into Groups

If you've got the time, consider breaking your attendees into groups to do some exercises. Whenever I have the opportunity to do this at events the evaluations are noticeably higher. I also think that retention is higher.

Try to keep your groups to between four and six members. Anything higher or lower doesn't work nearly as well. If you're using round tables, this is easy to do. If people are sitting theatre style or some other way, put the ball in their court.

Announce to the people that they must arrange themselves into groups in 30 seconds or less and not have more than 2 people from the same company or organization in one group. If you want, you can add other qualifiers. You could, for example, ask them to make sure they have both genders represented.

After you create the group in this manner, then have them choose a group leader. Give them the criteria to do this. Tell them that the group leader is the person who is the shortest member of the group or the youngest or the one with the darkest hair. It doesn't matter, just make choosing a leader easy.

If you stay in groups for extended periods, it's a good idea to switch group leaders every few hours, so as not to let one person monopolize the leadership role.

Use Exercises to Prove a Point

I've participated in a lot of seminars where the facilitator will have the attendees undertake an exercise that makes no sense. It might be fun and enjoyable, but it doesn't seem to make any sense or make a point related to the topic.

Don't follow this example. Make sure every exercise you do is not just interesting and amusing, but proves a point related to the information that you're delivering.

It's always better to have people discover the knowledge you want them to learn. Rather than giving out information or ideas in straight lecture form, give your group exercises where they will learn what you want them to know, on their own.

Doing this works much better because people get a greater sense of satisfaction if they are learning things on their own, rather than you just giving them the information. Study after study proves people remember longer that which they do themselves.

I've seen Fortune 500 company presidents down on the ground playing with Legos. Adults tend to learn best when they're learning like kids. Don't worry if you create an exercise that seems juvenile.

Frequent Breaks Pay Big Dividends

I went to a seminar a week before writing this section. It was a weekend seminar and the seminar leader went as long as two hours without giving us a break. Your bladder may be that strong, but your audience members need a break at a **minimum** of every 90 minutes. I prefer short mini-breaks every hour or so.

This is why most college classes run 50 minutes. People can't absorb more information than that at one time. Educators have determined this is the ideal length of time for people to assimilate information. Follow their lead.

If you have to cram a lot of information into a short period of time, I understand. I do the same. Just make sure to give people short breaks to keep their attention.

The biggest issue for most seminar leaders is getting people back into the room quickly when you do a break. You can get around this by training people early in your event. If you give your first break for "six minutes" make sure that you go out into the halls (if that's how you're set up) and give people a shout. Then start going at **exactly** six minutes from having announced your break, even if you have to shout at first to be heard over the din of people who are still on break. If you are giving people great information, people won't want to miss a minute of what you have to say.

If you ignore this rule you'll get hurt in evaluations and in product sales as well. Remember your over-riding goals: to get great evaluations and to sell a ton of product. Take breaks and keep people comfortable. It will keep people buying as well.

Dealing With People: The Good, The Bad, and the Annoying

Treating Attendees With Respect

The first principle of handling your attendees is to treat all people with the utmost respect.

Of course you should do this, right? It sounds obvious and it is. Let me give you a real-life example to illustrate this. I conducted a seminar for a continuing education center many years ago where only five people showed up. That's not a misprint. **Five** people.

Naturally, I was disappointed. Many people would have delivered less than a high-quality performance. I made sure to give people my best that evening. Little did I know that one lady in attendance was the publisher of a large magazine.

She proceeded to give me close to $8,000 in business over the next year. She later told me that the way I handled things that evening convinced her that I was the person to do the training for her people in-house. Do you think she would have hired me if I had delivered less than a quality performance?

The Distracted, Disinterested Attendee

You will be doing a seminar at some point in the future and someone in the crowd will look like they aren't interested. You will get bothered by this fact. Maybe they aren't giving you eye contact. Maybe they're sitting there reading a newspaper.

If you try to get this person to "like" you, you're wasting your time and energy. I was doing a speech in Charlottesville, Virginia, to a group of about 275 people. The topic was telephone skills. Exciting topic, right?

The audience was seated in a mini movie theatre with stadium seating. I was doing a one-day event and in the afternoon session I noticed three women who were seated on my far right hand and about halfway to the back.

They were talking among themselves and basically ignoring what I was doing. I spent the entire three hours talking to them. I looked at them and cajoled them with my eyes. Nothing I did seemed to get their attention or convince them to pay attention to what I was saying.

This is the last time I ever did this. Don't try to convert the unconvertible. Some people will pay attention, others will not. All you can do is deliver great information. You can't make your audience do anything they don't want to do. Learn this lesson early and save yourself a lot of grief.

Dealing With Difficult Attendees

Every once in a while you'll get a real pain in the butt at an event. The way that you handle these people is critical to your success. Here are some tips to deal with these folks effectively.

When a participant gets angry at you in front of your group, you'll never win if you shoot back with the same kind of response. Even if you "win," you've still lost. The audience perspective is that you hold the advantage. You're in front of the group and therefore have the most power.

If you win the argument, no matter who is at fault, you'll be perceived as the bad guy. You must keep your cool and deal with the issue they are presenting and not the emotion they are displaying. Do this right and you'll win your group over immediately. Do it wrong and you'll never recover.

Often at a seminar you'll encounter the person who wants to monopolize the floor with comments or questions. These people are either very smart and have a lot to contribute or they are just idiots who like to hear themselves talk.

With a person who has a lot to offer, pull them aside and tell them how valuable you think their contributions are. Let them know that because of time constraints you'd like them to give a brief presentation (usually five minutes or so) at some point late in the event.

This will keep them quiet and also give others the benefit of their knowledge.

I've learned to enlist the rest of the attendees in dealing with the person who talks incessantly with nothing really valuable to contribute. When this particular kind of person pipes up for the fourth time in the first hour, I just turn to the group and ask them if they would like to continue along the path that the individual is suggesting. Usually the group will turn on them and tell them to sit down and shut up. You don't have to do the dirty work, your audience will!

There are some people who will be so difficult you'll want to ask them to leave. At the first break after you make this determination, pull them to the side and suggest to them that this event isn't right for them. Tell them you'd be more than willing to give them a refund and send them on their way.

One negative, pain-in-the-ass participant can infect the entire group. Cut them out like a cancer as soon as possible.

Every once in a while you'll get someone who will actually try to harass you when you start your product pitch. They'll speak up and tell the group that they don't think it's appropriate for you to be pitching. If you've got a lot of people sitting in a room you could stand to lose thousands of dollars if you don't handle this properly.

I suggest you let the heckler finish their tirade. Then tell them that they are free to leave the room and take a break but you'd like to let other people know about the resources you've got to offer because many other people have found them to be valuable. After you've said that, continue with your pitch.

If they still won't behave, then they're a difficult attendee and you should gently but firmly ask them to leave at the first opportunity.

Handling Questions

When people ask questions during an event, you have two choices. You can either answer them on the spot or you can choose to defer the question until later.

If you do answer the question immediately, make sure it doesn't draw you too far off topic. If you choose to defer the question, do so respectfully. People will be ticked off if you don't answer the question eventually. In order to insure you get every question answered, here's what I recommend.

Put a big board at the back of the room. Give everyone sticky notes or 3x5 cards and push-pins. When they ask a question you can't or choose not to answer at a point in time have them write down the question and put it on the board.

At the breaks, pull off the notes. Answer them before you start into your regular speaking routine again. Doing it this way will encourage people to write down their questions immediately as they come up (so they won't be frustrated), but it will allow you to answer the questions when you feel it makes sense.

Always repeat questions when they are asked, unless there are just five or six of you sitting around a conference table and you're not taping the presentation.

There are three main reasons why you need to do this. First, you have to make sure that everyone in the audience hears what the question was. Second, unless the audience is miked, people listening to your seminar on tape won't hear the question. Third, you need to give your mind a few minutes to formulate a response.

Record Everything You Do

Record everything you do. I have been guilty of not doing this myself on occasion. It was a mistake. Why? There are a number of reasons.

First, you need to be able to critique yourself. If you get your evaluations back and you find that people didn't particularly like what you said or did, you can go back and review the tape.

Second, you may be able to sell the recording, either now or in the future. Not recording your events may end up losing a lot of revenue.

Would you ever want to record an event that is essentially a duplication of an earlier event? You might. Why would anyone buy these tapes if they already owned the first set? Some people would be willing to buy these tapes even if they have a recording of basically the same event already to hear the audience questions (which are always different) and your answers. They also think that they may pick up something different. Perhaps they will. Maybe not in substance, but in style. Why disappoint them? They are willing to pay for this information. Give it to them.

Third, you may capture a "magic moment" on tape. What is a magic moment? This is where you do or say something to your audience that brings the house down. They either laugh or cry or explode with applause and adulation. You want to have this on tape. Take all of the magic moments and cut them together and you will have a phenomenal demo video or audio that you can use to promote yourself as a speaker and seminar leader.

Fourth, if for some reason you sell twice as much stuff from the platform one day, you'll want to know why. You won't know unless you go back and carefully examine your pitch.

Fifth, you need to critique yourself.

Bottom line? Record everything. A pain in the ass? You betcha. Worth doing? Absolutely.

Trust me. When you end up capturing a magic moment on tape you'll call me to tell me how glad you were that it was being recorded.

Basic Audio-Video Equipment Advice

I own my own equipment for audio and video taping my events. By the time you rent this stuff a few times, you've paid for it. If you do a few events a year in your home city, it will quickly pay for itself.

The big hassle is transporting loads of equipment across the country. Therefore, whatever equipment you buy, make sure it's portable. For special events you may need some pretty fancy equipment, but for everyday use all you'll need is a quality audio recorder and a decent DV camera.

Please don't make the same mistake I did on this one. I have produced many audio and video cassette training programs. For many years I produced exclusively audio programs. I never bought a good audio recording device. This was a huge mistake.

Don't follow my lead. Bite the bullet and buy a nice recording device and a good mike. I use a Marantz deck. I also bought a $100 mike. The total was about $450. The net result if you do things this way will be a good clean "master" of your presentation.

You will then be able to duplicate it "as is" or edit the final product. Trust me on this one. Spend the money now. You will make your money back when you sell your first set of audio tape products. This is well worth it. Do it!

I suggest you get your audio equipment through a company called Kingdom. (Contact information is in Appendix A in the "Million-Dollar Rolodex.") They sell a variety of audio and video related materials. They primarily target religious organizations, but they will sell to "secular" groups as well. They are an amazing organization. Their sales staff is very knowledgeable and their service is first rate. I

highly recommend that anything that you need in the audio-visual arena, you check with them first.

At those events that I have in my home city of Las Vegas, I occasionally use a better DV camera with three chips in addition to my lower-end camera. Besides having three chips (which means you get a clearer picture and better color) it also allows you to have multiple camera angles. The better one also has a better lens. This can be very helpful in putting together a demo video, which could be deadly boring if everything was shot from the same angle. Unless you're going to be using the video for broadcast purposes, there's no need to pop for an expensive, high-end unit.

Let's talk about video tape products. There are some really crappy videos floating around out there. I have been to numerous seminars given by supposed gurus in the field of information product marketing who disagree with me, but I believe you must have a decent-looking product to sell.

This doesn't mean you have to spend enough to produce a Hollywood-style video. It should be somewhere between that point and looking like you did the video on your personal camcorder.

I don't want you to spend big money on video productions. I **do** want you to spend enough money to impress those who buy your video enough that they will buy more. They must be most impressed with the **content** of the video. But we don't want them to be distracted by inferior production value.

Unless you know a lot about video production, **don't** try and do it yourself. Contact me and I'll give you some pointers to people who can help.

Don't Allow Attendees to Tape Your Seminar

Don't ever allow participants to tape the seminars you do. You need to have this policy in writing on your handout materials. You also need to mention it at the beginning of the seminar when you do your housekeeping spiel. You don't want people to tape you for three reasons.

First, you want to sell products to them.

Second, you own the copyright to your material. If you allow people to copy that material freely, you risk the copyright itself.

Third, the quality of your recorded word will be suspect. Let's assume that someone shows up at your seminar with a walkman. They tape your seminar. The tapes get handed around. The quality of the sound will probably be lousy. This will make you look bad.

Take Notes While Giving the Seminar

Participants will improve your seminar each time you give it. That is, if you let them.

The key is to keep an instructors manual open next to you. This is a seminar workbook or manual that you keep as your copy every time you do a seminar.

As you go through the seminar, make notes in the appropriate area of the workbook. As you do more and more seminars, you will make changes as a result of participant feedback. Your seminar will get better and better with each seminar that you do.

By the time you have given the seminar 30 times, changes will be minimal, but you'll still get an occasional great idea, so keep your pen handy at all times!

From the Podium: Making a Smooth Product Pitch

OK, with the seminar goods delivered, it's time for you to switch hats from seminar leader to product pitch person. There are lots of ways and thoughts about the best approach to this.

When I was doing seminars for CareerTrack they insisted that I follow their system of transitioning from the seminar to the pitch. They suggested that I do this song and dance that made it look like smooth "flow" from content to sales pitch. For the most part I didn't listen to them!

Transition from Presentation to Product Pitch

When I get to the point where I want to let people know about my products that are for sale, I say: "Ok, folks, now's the time for my two-minute commercial."

I never try and "slip the pitch in." People are too intelligent for that to work. Everyone knows you're trying to sell them. So tell them. Don't BS them.

Timing of the Product Pitch

The length of your program determines where the pitch should occur. If you're doing a presentation of less than two hours, pitch when you've got about 10% of your material left to deliver.

If you're doing a three-hour presentation with a lot of content, you can pitch right before your break which should be scheduled halfway through. If you're doing a one-day seminar, pitch just before lunch.

The earliest you should **ever** pitch is half way through an event. This gives you the opportunity to establish credibility with your audience.

Making the Pitch Professionally

When to Display Your Products

Don't display your products before the event gets started. If you do, people will be braced for the pitch before it even comes. Keep your products up in front of the room until you pitch. Only after you've pitched should you move the products out from behind a curtain or out from under the table and display them. Never do it before you've pitched but it's alright to hold them up and show them during the pitch.

Picking Up and Referring to Product During Seminar

During your seminar, create a valid excuse to physically pick up one or more of your products. For example, you can find a need to look something up in one of the manuals. Don't do this more than once or twice. Try to use this technique for greatest impact after being asked a question.

Should You Have a Visual in Your Presentation For Your Products?

Some people will put up a visual aid, often a copy of the order sheet, to help them pitch their products. I normally don't do this. My suggestion is that you test it. If you use a lot of other visuals, it makes more sense that you would use one for your product presentation.

There is no way to know what the definitive answer is to this question until you test. Testing will help you figure out what works best.

Don't Show Your Video

If you sell any videos, don't give into the inevitable temptation to show them or even excerpts from them. All it can do is hurt you. If you've established credibility they will buy without seeing it. Showing the video will only give them a reason **not** to buy. But, the videos had better be good or you'll get them back.

Don't Sell Your Book!

That's right, I said, "Don't sell your book." Why? It's your lowest-priced item (or one of them). People who feel some sort of obligation to buy **something** from you will be able to do so without spending any serious money on your **real** content products.

I always tell people who ask if they can buy my book, "I'm sorry, but I only bring enough books to the seminar to provide as bonuses to people who buy one of the larger packages. You can get the book online at Amazon.com or special order it through your local book-store if you like."

When to Hand Out Product Order Sheets ... And When NOT To

Whenever I attend a speech or seminar I am amazed at how many speakers attach an order sheet for their products to their handout. In most cases, this is the wrong way to do things. You lose control of the timing.

I never put the order sheet into peoples' materials or leave it on the chairs if I can avoid it. I don't want them to have the chance to look at things and make up their minds before I want them to or simply to ignore it.

I want the control.

If I am in a small group, I hand them out myself as I say the line: "Now here's the two-minute commercial." I say this as I am handing out the order sheets one by one to seminar attendees.

If I am in a larger group and have some assistants, I ask them to hand out the order sheets when I give them some kind of a sign. Then, I don't begin doing my product presentation until just about everyone has an order form in their hands. If you do this quickly and efficiently it will work.

You do not want to have people sitting there going over the order sheet for a minute or two until you lead them through what they have just read. Again, you need to control the timing to make this work.

If you are fortunate to give a presentation to a group of over 1,000 people this becomes impractical. You'll probably have to attach the order sheet to the handout.

*B*ack of the Room: Getting Them to Buy Your Products

You've finished the seminar. You've left them gasping with delight at your content. You've given them a clear sales pitch. Now it's time to close in for the kill ... er, sale.

The Mental Side of Product Sales

There is a psychological or mental side to the selling process, regardless of whether it takes place at the back of your seminar room or in a client's office or over the Web. Here are some basic things to remember about this aspect of selling.

You Must LOVE Your Products

Unless you **love** your products, it will be very difficult to sell them. Why? Because you'll be thinking that you're scamming people when you get into your pitch.

In order to feel confident in your products you have to be happy with both their content and the packaging. If you aren't happy with either of these, it will be tough to pitch them. Give it your all when you create them and package them attractively and you'll be fine.

Unless you think your stuff is great, you're dead. You've got to have absolute confidence in what you're selling and in the positive impact it can have on your customers. If you don't feel that way, go back and redo your products.

If you have that confidence you can even "rail" on people to buy. Why? Because you know it's good for them.

Be Confrontational of the Status Quo

To be successful selling your products, you must attack conventional wisdom. If you don't, you'll be perceived the same as everyone else in your field. If you're not different from the others, what's the compelling reason to buy anything from you?

Attack all the sacred cows you can. Go out on a limb if you truly believe something. State your case forcefully. Some people may be turned off by this approach, but those who aren't will be much more inclined to buy.

I love competition and I sometimes go head-to-head against them by name in my selling process. That gets peoples' attention. If you have the best product in your category, say so. If someone asks you specifically how you're better than so-and-so's seminar, tell them.

Make Them Like and Respect You

In order for people to buy from you two things must be true. They must like you and they must respect you.

Pick up a copy of Robert Cialdini's book *Influence* to understand the "power of liking." This book is also a great reference tool for understanding some other key elements of product sales. I highly recommend that you buy it and read it more than once. (One speaker at a recent bootcamp of mine told the audience to buy it and read it **seven times**.)

To make this happen you can't talk down to people but you must command their respect. The only way I've found to do this is to do your homework and present yourself articulately.

Understand their Lifetime Value

Lifetime value refers to the amount of money a customer will likely spend with you over the lifetime of their relationship with you. This is one reason it pays to treat people well — **all** the time. They have the potential to put a lot of money into your pocket.

How do you know the lifetime value of a customer? Here's a little exercise I recommend you do soon and repeat every few months. Add up the total number of seminar attendees you've had at a given event (or at the aggregate of all your events) over a year. Add up every dollar all those attendees have spent with you: seminar registration fees, other product, consulting fees, the whole nine yards. Now divide the total dollars by the total number of attendees.

If, for example, you find you've had 1,000 people attend your seminar during the past year and they've spent an aggregate total of $100,000, then the lifetime value of a customer for that seminar is $100. Knowing this figure can help you make intelligent decisions about customer acquisition strategies and costs, among other things.

11 Mistakes to Avoid

This section presents some of the most valuable content in this entire book. Read it. Memorize it. (OK, you don't have to memorize it. But it might help!) These are easily the 11 most common mistakes made by people who are unsuccessful in sales of their products.

1. Don't overpitch your products. Sell, but don't oversell.
2. Don't speak or cover material slowly. Going quickly helps sales.
3. Don't forget to include the benefits of your product in your sales presentation.
4. Don't forget to record every single presentation you make.
5. Don't forget to be confrontational of conventional wisdom.
6. Don't forget to measure your results every time you speak..
7. Don't let any product leave your office unless you are 100% satisfied with the content.
8. Don't wait to get the product absolutely perfect. Get going now.
9. Don't forget that you can sell other peoples' products until you create your own.
10. Don't forget to make people an irresistible offer.
11. Don't feel embarrassed to call me for coaching.

Working the Table

If you have a small group of 20 or 30 people, you can handle the sale of products yourself. I do. Collect the orders whenever people hand them to you and tell people that you will get the products to them at the end of the day. Or at the end of the session, however long it might be.

If you have more than 30 or so people, it will be wise to have someone else work the product table with you or instead of you (freeing you up to schmooze). You now have two choices. You can have your own people (temporary employees or people you work with regularly) work the tables or you can have volunteers working the table.

If you are working with an association, they are either tolerating your sale of products or they are fully supportive. If they are tolerating your sale of products, you will probably have to hire a temp to help you work the table. It usually isn't cost effective (depending on the size of the group) to fly in an employee. This of course depends on the number of people, your closing ratio, and the price points of your products. If you're not figuring on selling $10,000 worth of product at the seminar, you probably won't be able to justify bringing an assistant with you.

If you are doing a presentation with an organizations' or associations' blessing, chances are good that they will give you some staff to help you.

Some Selling Tips

Have Products in Inventory

People hate to pay for something and not be able to take it with them. Whenever you do an event make sure that you have product ready for them to take when they order. If you can't have everything, make sure you have at least one component of every package that people can take with them when they order. Of course if your products are all delivered digitally, you probably won't need to carry CDs or disks with them on it. In that case, though, you might want to consider giving buyers an instruction sheet for how to get the products and perhaps a password if one is in order.

If you are doing large events and offer people an A, B or C option you'll need to have packages prepared and ready to give them quickly when they approach your table. If you run out, make sure you have at least one item you can give to people

When you get back to your office after a seminar, fill your unfilled orders immediately. There is nothing that amuses me more when I'm watching an ad on TV than when they say: "Please allow 4–6 weeks for delivery." Why? This is absurd. Ship out the products as soon as you receive the order.

If, for some reason, you can't get the products out, call people and let them know. Keep them informed. Also, because it's your problem, offer them a freebie of some sort.

Creating an Order Sheet

Your order sheet should be designed so it is easy to understand and easy to buy. When you're done putting it together, hand it to a fourth grader and see if they can understand what the offer is and how to fill out the order sheet. If they can't, redo it until they can.

Group all the audios together if that makes sense. In most cases you'll be selling packages. List package A's components and then underneath it list package B. Package B will be all of the elements in A plus some additional items.

Describing Your Products' Features and Benefits

When you list what's in your products, make sure and include the features as well as the benefits. People don't buy a feature, they buy what that feature can do for them. You need to point out very clearly and concisely how a given feature can help them. Go through your description fairly quickly, but highlight the major benefit or benefits of each product.

How to Reduce Return Rates

Returns happen when you sell products. You just want to keep them as low as possible. How do you do this? The first and best answer is to create high-content products, with information which helps your customers immediately implement ideas you present.

Also, provide them with bonuses that once used they would feel embarrassed to return your products. The best thing I've found to use for this purpose is consulting time. Once they take you up on it, very rarely will they return the product and request a refund.

Record Your Product Pitches

I mentioned earlier the need to tape your presentations. Make sure that you tape all of your product presentations as well. This is your bread and butter. You need to analyze when you do well and when you fail so that you can look for patterns and continually improve your pitches.

Aids to Closing Sales

Free Additional Gifts, If ...

"Piling on" is a common selling practice in which you give people one final incentive to order now. I usually tell people that if they write the number "2" in the right hand corner of the order sheet and hand it to my assistants before they leave the room I'll give them 2 special gifts free. But they must hand in the order sheet **now**.

If people leave your event and don't order, the chances of them ordering are slim to none. Give them every incentive you can to get them to order on the spot. If you don't get them there, it's unlikely they will buy later.

Installment Selling

In some markets I will let people make three installment payments. This can dramatically increase sales in some markets. The only way to know is to test it. If you do use the payment system, don't let them take all the product. Give them something to start and then ship additional items as they make their payments.

Who Needs the Money?

If people get the feeling that you need the money when you pitch your products, you're dead. I usually use the line: "If you don't buy my products here today it won't substantially affect my financial position, but if you don't buy them, it may severely affect **your** financial position."

You don't have to use the same line, just make sure that you communicate this fact to your attendees or you'll have a potential problem.

One Great Pitch: It Hasn't Been Your Fault. Now It Is

The products you pitch should be helping people solve a problem. But we don't want them to feel stupid for not doing things "right" before coming to our seminar. Let them know that it's not their fault that they've been doing things "bass-ackwards" until now. Remind them that if they continue to do this stupid stuff now that they know better, it **will** be their fault.

Answer Their Questions Fully and Completely

Every once in a while I attend a seminar myself and see some nitwit speaker who doesn't fully answer a question in hopes of coercing someone to buy their products. **This is a terrible move**. Not only will people be pissed off at you, they will buy less. This strategy makes no sense. Answer all questions that they ask you fully and completely. They'll think there's more anyway.

To collect your free gift (worth $77) send an email to tips@seminarexpert.com

Questions about your products will come up at three points in time.

The first is before the presentation. Second is during the presentation. The final time might occur after the presentation itself. Depending on when the question is asked, your answer should be different. Let's go through this important area and how to handle questions at the various points.

Before the Presentation: When people ask about the products before my presentation, it can happen at two separate points in time. One point would be at the very beginning of the day (or presentation) with few, if any, people around. If this happens, give people a very brief description of the products. Then tell them you will be happy to give them a more complete description after you describe the products to the whole group.

If people approach you regarding products before the beginning of your presentation and quite a few other people are milling around, tell them you will be giving a complete description of the materials later on in the day. You don't want to look cheesy by presenting your products while people are all around and you haven't yet delivered anything of value. You will steal your own thunder.

During the Presentation: If someone interrupts your product sales presentation to ask a question, give them a quick answer and then keep going through your routine. You don't want to interrupt your flow. It will hurt your numbers if you interrupt your presentation for anything other than to answer a quick question. Answer quickly and keep going.

After the Presentation: If someone asks a question after the presentation, answer it fully but concisely. If an additional question comes out of the group, say the following: "I promised the commercial would only go two minutes. I would be happy to answer any of your questions one-on-one at the break. Would that be OK?"

Keep Sending them Information

Keep mailing and emailing to people who have attended your events. Some percentage of them, particularly those who bought something at the seminar, will continue to buy after the fact. If they liked what you had to say, they may not buy that product, but they may buy from you eventually. It's worth staying in contact with them.

Creating More Sales Right Now

There are only a few things I do really well. Selling products is definitely one of them. I sell more products from the platform than anyone that I have seen including some of the "great ones."

The information that I've compiled in this section of the book is a greatly condensed version of my book *Selling Products from the Platform*. If you like what you read here, you may want to pick up a copy of that book.

Successful speakers and seminar leaders often make much more than 50% of their revenue from product sales. If this concept is repugnant to you, **get over it**!

The only reason you should have a problem selling your products is if they aren't worth it. If that's the case, go back and redo them. If you've got great products that give people good value, then sell them with the zeal of a Baptist preacher.

If your products are great, the world needs to know.

Selling products at your seminars and other events is not optional. You must do it if you're going to be a successful seminar leader.

This means that first, you must have products to sell. If you don't, please pick up a copy of my book *Creating and Selling Information Products*.

This is an area I've learned how to do really well. Please read carefully. This section will be worth a lot of money to you over the next several years.

Upselling at the Product Table

You can significantly add to your numbers by having an effective upsell at the product table. When people come up to make a purchase, make them an offer to buy a more expensive product and make it an offer they can't refuse.

When people come up to your product table, you know that are ready to buy. Why not offer them a slight "bump" in what they were initially willing to pay? I think that a bump of just under $50 makes sense. If someone is coming up to buy your $197 package, offer them something that normally sells for $150 or more on its own for an additional $47.

Whatever deal you decide to present, make sure you have an upsell at the table that is so attractive that few people will turn you down.

Remember, your costs are so low that if you sell something for $47 that costs you $7 you're still making an additional $40 you didn't have.

Remember: "Do you want fries with that?" works for McDonald's. It also works for product sales.

Getting an Association on Your Side to Help Sell Products

If you're doing a presentation for an association, try to get them on your side and you'll sell a heck of a lot more product. One of the easiest ways to do this is to cut them in on a piece of the action. Offer to "kick them back" 15–20% of the sales you make. Use this system and many associations and their leaders will become your greatest salespeople. Many times the sales I make more than compensate for the fees I've been paid to attend the event. That's one of my favorite things on the planet: a complete win-win arrangement.

Additional Prodding

After you pitch your products, you can do some additional prodding to get people to buy. The problem is that it must be subtle so it doesn't appear to be over-selling.

If I'm doing a one-day seminar, I'll make my major pitch at lunch. I will then briefly remind people that they must get their order sheets in before the end of the day to get the discount right before the first afternoon break.

I will make up a question that I'll claim that someone asked me at the break about a product before I let the group go.

Anything more than this would be too much

Create Urgency

When you are selling your products, you always need to make people a special offer if they buy from you on the spot.

Your audience may have good intentions and think that they will eventually make a purchase from you, but for the most part, it's not going to happen. People have other things to buy. Unless you get them at that moment, you're highly unlikely to sell them later.

Sure, I'll describe a campaign you should use to get them to buy after the fact, but it won't be nearly as cost effective as getting them to dig into their wallet right there and then.

You may be successful in eventually converting some people in the future, but look at those sales as gravy.

Try to imagine that, unless you get 100% of your audience to buy, you will be executed after your presentation. How will your appeal go then? What would you say to try and convince people?

*F*rom the Podium: The End of the Seminar ... and Beyond

Evaluations: A Must-Do

At the end of each seminar/speech or workshop you do, you must hand out an evaluation. You need numerical feedback with regards to your presentation. You also need to find a way to get some great testimonials to use in future marketing efforts.

Evaluations give you a way to quantify your results. Using this data you can create certain data to help you promote your events. I will often say that the average rating for my events is a 9.6 on a scale from 1 to 10. You also need to ask people what they liked best and what they liked least about the presentation. This will help you improve the future events.

You need another section in which you ask people if they would be interested in certain kinds of additional services. The list of services you give them can comprise not only products and services you now have but those you are contemplating creating. When you review the evaluations, follow up quickly on these expressions of interest in other products. They represent a clear opportunity for additional revenue from a source that is favorably pre-disposed in your direction.

If you get people to write really great stuff about you, you also want to get them to sign off at the end of the evaluation so you can use the quotations in future promotional literature. Check the sample in Appendix A.

If you use any quotations, make sure you have the signed evaluations on file. There is a chance you may be called upon to produce them. I never have, but I always have them ready to produce, just in case.

Don't be thrown off if you get one person who really slams you in an evaluation. Chances are you pushed their buttons and they are just venting. The only time this is a concern is when you get more than an isolated occurrence of this kind of response.

Creating Your Next Seminar Audience

The easiest person to sell is an existing customer. The easiest product to sell your attendees is the advanced version of the seminar you're doing.

People who tend to buy one way, tend to continue to buy in that manner. If they "bought" your first seminar they'll be more apt to sign up for a seminar than anything else.

Pitch people on the upcoming event with an incentive for signing up today. Give them a significant bonus if they sign up on the spot. That way you've got the money in the bank and then you're on track to do the advanced seminar.

Make sure to differentiate the event. It can't be the same event given twice. You need to elaborate on your initial event.

Marketing costs are extremely low because you're mainly promoting to attendees at your current event. It's a no-brainer because you can usually charge more for the advanced event and you have no cost to promote to an existing seminar member.

You'll also get an idea as to whether an advanced seminar will work if people will actually register right then and there. If a bunch of people sign up, you'll have good evidence that the idea works.

After the Seminar

Don't leave immediately after your event. Stay around and hold court. Answer questions and give people more great insights. If they like what you have to say , it's likely they will buy more product. Speakers who immediately cut out at the end of their events are misguided.

Assessing Success by the Numbers

Every promotional method you use costs something. The simplest way to compute the success of your efforts is to use the "dollars out versus dollars in" method. Every marketing method you use to promote your event will have a different rate of return.

Here's how to compute effectiveness. Forget about expenses for this system. Simply take the number of dollars generated by registrations and compare that to the amount of money paid for the promotion or advertising. Let's say you spend $1,000 and make $2,000. That's a 2:1 return on investment, which is average. Below this ratio would be poor. If a particular marketing methodology pulled 3:1, then it would fall into the good category. Any method of promotion that pulled 4:1 or better is a home run!

If you had two promotions that pulled the exact same number of people, you would obviously go after those people with the promotional approach that cost the lesser amount of money.

You should use every promotional means that pulls more than it costs. In some cases, where you know you'll sell a boatload of products or consulting work, you may even be willing to use those methods that **don't** break even.

If you know through experience that your average attendee's lifetime value is $750, you should be willing to pay up to that amount (or some substantial portion of it) to get someone to attend your event.

But we also know that different people respond to different means of promotion. Some people will never respond to a solicitation made via TV. Others never respond to direct mail. You often will get a very different group of people from different kinds of promotion.

This simplistic approach works fine unless you sell products at your seminar. (And if you don't, you've kind of missed the whole point of this book, haven't you?) Unless you include product sales in your calculations, there is no way to tell how well you're doing. I recommend you use a measurement of Dollars/Person/Minute, as I explained in Chapter 4.

*O*utside the Seminar: Year-Round Selling

Selling in the "Real" World (Offline)

Although it's changing, the majority of products are still sold off-line. This will change as more and more products are able to be delivered on-line.

Right now, it's easy to deliver eBooks on-line. That's not the case with long-form audios and videos. The amount of bandwidth they require digitally is enormous. Most people are still using relatively slow (56K baud modem) connections to the Internet. But higher-speed systems are taking hold. When bandwidth and delivery speed reach an appropriate level and are sufficiently widely available, I would guess that virtually every product you sell will be digitally delivered.

Until that day comes, however, you must understand how to sell your products off-line. You'll need to learn how to produce such things as:

- a great sales letter
- compelling bonuses
- catalogs
- fax order sheets

You'll also want to have a toll-free number where people can more easily give you their money for your products.

A Great Sales Letter

To sell your products off-line you'll need a great sales letter. This is a necessity. If you've created one for your Web site, and it's working, you can use the same one, but be sure to remove Web-specific instructions like "click here" or "send me an email." If you need help in writing an effective sales letter, I have some recommendations for you in Appendix A.

Compelling Bonuses

No matter how good your front-end product is, you'll need some **killer** bonuses to help make it sell. I suggest you develop a number of very targeted and specific reports as well as a great single cassette audio and short video.

The reason you want to provide three types of bonuses goes back to the way people learn. Some people will want to read, others to listen and still others will want to watch. Your bonuses should be geared to attract each type.

The key to successful bonuses is to create highly useable content with great titles to make people want them. Many times people will buy your products just to get the bonuses you offer.

Catalog

In general, it's **not** a good idea to offer people a ton of different options too early in the selling process. Once they become a customer, it's permissible to send them a catalog of all of your products and services. This catalog should list everything that you offer in that niche and give people discounts for purchasing more than one item. The most important thing to remember when putting together your catalog is that you'll want it to be packed with benefits.

Fax Order Sheet

Many people like to use their faxes to order products off-line. To make this as easy as possible, create a fax order form that is simple and easy to follow. Make it simple enough for a fourth grader to figure out.

Always include an upsell on the order sheet itself. Done correctly, as many as 20% or more of your customers will go for the upsell. Make the price of the upsell approximately 20% of the value of your primary sale.

If your product sells for $100, offer your customer an upsell of a product that would normally sell for more but which you'll make available now for just $19.95. The best way to do this is to simply ask people to put an "X" in a box if they want the product that you're offering. Come up with two or three lines to highlight the benefits of this product and you're off to the races. If at all possible, make it a digitally delivered product to reduce your costs. If you opt for something else, consider a single cassette tape which is inexpensive to produce and to ship.

Toll Free Number

A toll free number for selling off-line is essential. Many people still try to get by without one. I don't recommend it. If you're following my advice, you'll make plenty of money from the sales of your products and services to justify the cost of a toll-free phone number.

If at all possible, have a live person answer the phone during normal business hours. People expect that. If necessary, do it yourself or find someone to help you out in exchange for a percentage of every sale.

Conclusion

Although it would be nice to do all of your business on-line, I don't think it will ever happen. Just as people will always want to attend a live seminar or workshop, some people will still want to buy products they can feel and touch. You should be prepared to supply them with both.

Online Selling Techniques

If you're following my advice, you're recording all of your seminars. You will want to sell the audio and video tapes of those seminars. One of the ways to sell these items is online, over the Internet.

With all of your products, you'll be able to **sell** them online, but you'll only be able to **deliver** eBooks and other electronically stored products online. Such products can include newsletters or eZines, software, database access, membership (e.g., in an online community where they can get coaching help), and others.

To sell your products effectively online you'll need to follow a simple system.

Step 1

Before you do anything, you'll want to talk to a search engine specialist like my friend Kimberly Judd (kjudd@cybermarkint.com). She will help you make decisions on what to name your site and your business. This must be done **before** you do anything else. A bad decision in this area will have serious negative consequences. Don't skip this step.

Step 2

Set up your business officially. This entails at least two steps: forming the legal entity and obtaining appropriate licenses. If you're setting up a sole proprietorship, you'll need to file a "doing business as" (DBA) with your county. If you choose to incorporate, you'll need to talk to a lawyer to set up your incorporation documents. Nevada is a great state in which to incorporate regardless of where you live or where your company's offices are located. My attorney, Mace Yampolsky, can be reached at 720-807-5777. Make sure and tell him I sent you. Another good contact for this kind of advice is Al Allen at 800-254-5779.

In most communities, you'll be required to pay a fee and obtain a business license. Check both your city and your county offices to determine what is needed in your area and then comply with the rules. Lots of people are tempted to skip this step but it can be really embarrassing down the road.

Step 3

Next, you'll need to register your domain name. I use www.enom.com. They charge $8.95 per year per domain name if you buy lots of domains. If you don't buy lots of domains, email me and I'll get you set up with a special account so you'll still get the $8.95 rate. These folks also have great customer service. I highly recommend them.

Step 4

The most important step in creating your Web site is to write the copy for the site itself. Do it right and the money will start rolling in. If you have a site that can close more than 3% of all unique visitors you're doing extremely well. If you aren't very good or don't have the time to write the copy for your site, check Appendix A of this book for recommendations on copywriters.

Step 5

The first element of your system will be your Web site. At that Web site your prospects will find the sales letter we just talked about.

You'll also want to have a pop-up window come up when people leave your site without having placed an order. See Appendix A for some thoughts about where to get the scripts that will allow you to do this. There are lots of pre-built scripts for this purpose. This pop-up window should make them a great offer to get them to opt-in to your list. Offering them some kind of a special digitally delivered report on a topic of interest with a compelling title will usually work.

Remember your goal is to get people either to buy your product or to opt-in to your list. If they merely opt-in to your list, you'll want to devise a series of auto-responder messages to convince them to buy your front end product.

To sell on-line you'll need a merchant account (so you can take and process credit card orders) and an Internet gateway account (which somehow connects the merchant account and a bank but don't ask me how!). To make it easy for people to purchase, you must have a shopping cart program.

To handle all of the functions described above, I recommend you use a single program like WebMarketingMagic (www.webmarketingmagic.com). I helped formulate the components for this product, which includes an eBook module.

I use WebMarketingMagic to do all of the things I suggest you do above. This program will give you everything you want in one place. You **could**, if you were so inclined, find all of the components in other places. You'd then have a lot of other vendors and have to integrate all of the components yourself.

Unless you're a real computer geek (and I envy you if you are), then get WebMarketingMagic. It's fully integrated to do everything you need. It's also very affordable. It's easy to set up and can be used by anyone, regardless of how computer illiterate you are.

Making your products available to people on-line will produce orders from people who attend your events and those who don't. Many people will tell others about your products and many will go to your Web site. This will produce orders.

Step 6

Start up-selling people to other products (yours and others) both on and off-line. This can be done using your auto-responders as well as traditional direct mail pieces.

Getting Them to Buy Your Consulting Services

If you provide consulting services to your clients, this is probably your highest-ticket item. It may also be high-margin, though it is also labor-intensive and may not fit your lifestyle. If you do want to convert some of your information product buyers into consulting clients, this section provides an overview of how to do that.

Obviously, we can only do so much in the limited space we have here. If you're really interested in this topic, you should check out my seminar for consultants (see www.consultingexpert.com for details).

Using the Seminar to Sell Your Consulting Services

Seminars are a great way to trade your customers up to consulting. For some people, your seminar will be the first product they have bought from you. Others will have purchased other products before attending your event. In either case, the seminar gives you a chance to showcase both your speaking skills and your content knowledge.

There are other models for generating consulting business, but doing seminars is one of the easiest I know about.

The keys to generating consulting business are similar to those that lead to a great seminar experience.

First, you have to give people an incredible amount of useful information. This will convince them of your knowledge of the topic and your willingness to share it.

Second, you must never withhold information. If you ever give people the feeling that you are not giving them the "straight scoop" (i.e., that you are holding back to entice them to use you as a consultant), they will not respond well. In turn, they will be much less likely to give you consulting work.

Some seminar leaders/speakers think that if you keep a little bit of information in your back pocket people will pay extra in order for you to show your cards. Nothing could be further from the truth. People are much more likely to give you consulting business when you give them everything you know and respond to all questions fully and forthrightly.

If you do this, people will be much more likely to ask you to come and give them individual help. No matter how much information you provide, they will think you have more to give. When you deliberately and obviously hold back information, you risk having them feel "taken" by some kind of a ruse to get you to give them more money.

When someone asks you a question during your seminar and you respond with: "Well, hire me as a consultant and I'll give you all of the information that you want ... " you are dead in the water. People will feel taken advantage of. (The exception to this — and a great opportunity to sell your consulting during the seminar — is if an attendee asks a question that is so specific to his or her company or situation that it is obvious that nobody else will want to hear the answer.)

You need to be 100% willing to share everything you know during the seminar. You owe it to your participants. Behave this way and you'll get plenty of consulting work.

Insider Secrets to Consulting Success

In addition to the keys discussed in the previous section, you'll need to understand some other techniques to be successful at generating consulting business from your seminars.

Follow Up on Leads

When someone expresses interest in your consulting services, follow up quickly. This is definitely a case of striking while the iron is hot. Send them whatever information they request right away. After sending them the information they asked for, call them and see what else you can do.

Ask them for a specific time frame for when they might be interested in using you as a consultant. Asking them a question like this will help you figure out whether or not they are serious. Follow up on these leads regularly, but don't be too pushy.

Never Appear Too Hungry

Even though you need to follow up on everyone who contacts you, it's not a great idea to appear to be **too** eager. Whether you're talking to them over the phone or writing to them (email included), you can never appear too hungry for the business. The more you look like you need the business, the less chance you'll have of getting it.

You have to walk a fine line between being pleasantly persistent and appearing too hungry and **needing** the work.

Have the Information Ready:
Strike While the Iron is Hot!

You must have any and all promotional material to promote your consulting practice ready to go. When you make a contact that might have an interest in your services, the worst thing you can do is not have anything to send them.

What do you need? In addition to your products, you'll need a complete set of materials that are specifically geared to promoting your consulting business. This would include a few key items: a one-sheet summary of your services, references, perhaps a fee schedule if you have one. This information should be in your computer and ready to be delivered via email, fax and snail mail.

I do **not** suggest you have these items pre-printed. This will prevent you from customizing everything you send. I suggest you make minor changes to your one-sheet promotional to meet the needs of your prospective clients.

You'll also want to have plenty of testimonials about your services ready as well. To get these you'll need to ask for them. At the end of every consulting gig, ask your client if he or she will write a letter of recommendation describing what you did for them and what benefits they gained from your assistance.

Using Personal Contacts to Sell Consulting

I have used personal contacts to gain a lot of consulting clients. At the seminars, I try to befriend as many of the participants that I can. I'm lucky because I actually like people and this process comes easily to me. Those individuals who don't become clients will often become friends.

You may have a difficult time using this method. If it doesn't match your personality then don't try to force it. It will only come off as disingenuous.

Never Go Out Looking for Consulting Work

I do not recommend that you go out actively looking for consulting. This an outdated model for building a consulting business. Not only is it difficult, it is time-consuming and demeaning. Unless you are a well-known author in your field, the chances for success are limited to say the least.

Instead, use my system to attract people to you. Get them to enter your funnel by purchasing one of your products at a price point where they feel comfortable. Then, trade them up the ladder. Eventually, a certain number will call you for high-end consulting services.

Maintain Price Integrity

Discounting will hurt you in the long run. If you are just starting out, or if money is particularly tight one month, it will be tough not to want to discount. Please avoid doing this.

The only pricing adjustments I make are for entrepreneurs and non-profit organizations. This way I can legitimately present a two-tiered price structure. Let's say I charge standard corporate clients $4,500 a day. I would offer entrepreneurs and non-profits 50% off this rate.

In the event I have a corporate client who pleads poverty, I will sometimes give them the lower rate if they promise not tell anyone else and allow me to cut some of my basic services that I would usually provide. An example might be a final report that I would usually include. I would ask them if in exchange for the price reduction I could dispense with the final report. In most cases they will gladly agree.

Barring that, you might be able to get your client to let you reuse your consulting findings for him as a special report you can sell to others. Sometimes, they'll want you to give them exclusive access for some period of time (3–6 months is normal) so their competitors don't get their hands on the same information at a steep discount before they've had a chance to capitalize on it.

Be particularly wary of what my friend and colleague Dan Shafer calls the "soft-shoe two-step." A prospective client will say something like, "We don't have enough budget to pay your usual fee for this project, but if you'll give us a break on the price on this one, we'll show you that we're interested in building a long-term relationship. We'll give you lots of work later at your regular fee." That future work somehow never materializes.

When you do cut prices you will probably discover what I have over the years. The biggest pains in the neck are those people who nickel and dime you. Your full-fare customers are usually the easiest to deal with.

As more work comes your way you can be more selective. At this point, whenever I perceive a customer will be difficult I will frequently increase my rate by 50% or more. I figure if they are still interested, they are paying for their degree of difficulty.

P.S. The Bottom Line (Do NOT Skip Here Immediately!)

If you're like me you probably ignored the title of this chapter and skipped to here before reading the book. Shame on you! Yeah, right.

If you haven't yet read the book, you're in for an exciting journey. If you have read the book in logical order, you're now really just starting.

The seminar business is fascinating. There are many people making millions of dollars each year in the field. Perhaps you'll be one of them. Perhaps you **are** one of them!

There are some very important points that bear repeating before I'll feel like I've done my best for you. In my opinion, here are the most important elements you need to take with you.

Test small before you invest

Anyone who claims to know how a seminar on a certain topic will work in a certain market using a certain method of promotion is lying or mistaken. As an expert, I may have an inkling, but then again, I may be dead wrong.

That being the case, you need to test things on a small scale before you spend a lot of money to roll out a seminar tour. This might be frustrating at times. In your gut you might feel that you've got a sure winner. If so, it will stand up to testing.

Test your seminars on a small scale in a similar market to see if it works, then roll it out.

Albert Einstein has E=MC2.
Fred Gleeck has TR=SR+PS+CB

A true understanding of this formula will be the basis of all of your success in the seminar business.

There are many seminar operators who don't make a dime on the "front end" from registration dollars and make a boatload of money on the back-end in product sales and consulting business.

Keep track of your numbers and understand this formula. Remember to always look at CB (consulting business) as your gravy. Don't use it to make basic computations because consulting business may come in years after you do your seminar.

Create products and learn how to sell them

Every single successful seminar promoter I know makes a huge percentage of their income from the sale of their products. To sell products, you must create them. Learn how to put together great products and then learn the mechanics of selling them from the platform. Learn this well and you're on the road to making millions.

Mail to your in-house list regularly

If there is one mistake I've made in the past (and continue to make more often than I'd admit under torture) it's not mailing to my list often enough. Your in-house list is willing to hear from you regularly if you approach them with great offers. Don't be afraid of over-mailing to your list. It is virtually impossible to do.

Of course, before you can **mail** to your in-house list, you have to **have** an in-house list. I cannot over-emphasize the absolute necessity of creating, maintaining, managing, and using a database of prospects and clients as the core of your marketing program. With such a list, success is all but guaranteed; without it, it's going to be hard to succeed almost in spite of the quality of your products and offerings.

Give people much more than you promised and you'll be set

Most seminar providers do the bare minimum expected of them. You should do just the opposite. People should walk out of your events singing your praises at the top of their lungs to anyone who will listen. Generate this kind of "buzz" about your events and you'll never lack registrants. Under-promise and over-deliver with both your seminars and your products.

Finally, have a good time

When I imagine having fun while working I picture myself up in front of a group of people doing a seminar. If you don't feel that way yourself, you're probably in the wrong business.

Closing Thoughts

If you need my help, or would like to contact me, I'm busy, but available. I can help. Please feel free to call me to discuss how we might work together to create a great and highly profitable event. As opposed to other so-called gurus in a variety of fields, I **like** to hear from people. But don't be surprised if I suggest you buy something from me when you call. My "stuff" is good and I'm always anxious to recommend it where appropriate.

If you want to stay up-to-date with the latest concepts in the seminar field, make sure to send an email to tips@seminarexpert.com. This will put your name on my seminar list to receive the latest information about the seminar business.

So go out there and make millions of dollars doing seminars. If you make more than you expected to make as a result of this book, send me the difference!

*A*ppendix A

Other Valuable Learning Resources From Fred Gleeck

How to Self Publish Your Own Book, Get Famous and Make Well Over $250K a Year

This one-day seminar on audio-tape will give you a complete overview of the self-publishing process. It will provide you with everything you need to get your book written and printed AND start developing and marketing a back end line of other products and services.

For More info go to: www.SelfPublishingSuccess.com

Marketing and Promoting Your Own Seminar and Workshops

Whether you're a speaker, author or consultant, seminars can be a very attractive source of additional revenue. There's only one problem. You can lose a lot of money if you don't what you're doing. This program will show you exactly how to promote your own events and make money doing it. I've done over 1300 one-day events myself!

For More info go to: www.SeminarExpert.com

How to Make $5,000 a Day as a Professional Speaker

If you want to really make a living from professional speaking, you NEED this program. In a fast moving interview, Fred Gleeck reveals the secrets of how to get started and thrive as a speaking professional. Other programs may give you part of the story, this program gives you the whole story!

For More info go to: www.ProfessionalSpeakingSuccess.com

Creating and Selling Information Products

If you're an information marketer, you need to create information products to be truly successful. Not only will creating products enhance your image; it will also allow you to make money while you sleep. This program will show you how to turn your products into a solid money making machine that requires a minimum of effort.

For More info go to: www.SellingInfoProducts.com

How to Start and Build a Turbo-Charged Consulting Business

If you have expertise in a topic, you can get paid for that expertise as a consultant. Most consultants spend their time chasing down prospects that have no interest in their services. This one-day seminar on audio-tape will show you the right way to prospect for high dollar customers and get paid while you're doing it.

For More info go to: www.ConsultingExpert.com

24 Direct Marketing Secrets to Your Professional Services Business

If you market any service whatsoever, this is a program you can use. You'll get the inside secrets on how to do marketing that REALLY works. It's called direct marketing. It's the only kind of marketing I do. It's the only kind of marketing you'll want to do after you listen to this program. It's packed with highly relevant useable ideas.

For More info go to: www.DirectMarketingExpert.com

How to Double Your Sales on the Web in 90 Days or Less

If you want to make your website successful you have to do two things. First, you have to design a site that REALLY sells. Secondly, you have to find an effective way to drive traffic to your site. The problem is that most people don't truly know how to do either effectively. This program will show you how to do both!

For More info go to: www.WebMarketingSolution.com

How to Get Your Own Radio Show in 7 Days or Less

If you'd like to host your own radio show, you can! In this audio program I interview Mike Litman on how to get your own radio show in under a week. YOU can be on the radio in a fraction of the time you thought possible following these step by step instructions.

For More info go to: www.GetYourOwnRadioShow.com

How to Make ANY Product an Amazon Best Seller

If you'd like to turn your book, audio or video into an Amazon best seller, this is the program for you. You'll learn the inside secrets to catapult your product onto the top of the Amazon charts.

For More info go to: www.CreateYourBestSeller.com

How to Start Your Own Association

Starting your own association will give you tons of benefits. Among them, you can appoint yourself the president and get instant credibility in your field. This program will show you how to do virtually everything to do just that.

For More info go to: www.StartYourOwnAssociation.com

How to Run Your Own Conferences

Want to create and market your own conferences? This is the program that will show you how. I interview a top expert in the field and get him to "spill the beans" on exactly how to run highly profitable conferences and large events.

For More info go to: www.RunYourOwnConferences.com

Writing Effective Web Copy

Want to get your web copy to close a higher percentage of visitors to do what you want? It's tough, but you'll learn how to do exactly that in this fast moving interview of internet marketing maven, Terry Dean.

For More info go to: www.WebCopyMagic.com

Creating Highly Profitable Joint Ventures

Joint ventures are how many people have made their fortunes. You too can learn the secrets to making them work for you as well. This fast paced interview with Terry Dean will give you the formula for success with JV's.

For More info go to: www.JointVentureGenius.com

Info Products Bootcamp

This 22 hour audio program will give you everything you need to start and build a successful information products business. If you have specific knowledge in your field, why not package and get paid for it?

For More info go to: www.InfoProductsSeminar.com

Seminar on Seminars Bootcamp

Want to market and promote your own seminar? This 3 day information packed event on audio will show you exactly how to do it yourself. Soup to nuts, this program will walk you through the seminar business from A to Z.

For More info go to: www.SeminarOnSeminars.com

Making Big Money Using Google

Learn how to use Google and specifically Google Ad words to drive loads of traffic to your site. This fascinating interview with Perry Marshall will give you everything you need to succeed.

For More info go to: www.TheGoogleExpert.com

For the latest products that I offer, please go to www.FredGleeck.com. This site will give you the latest listings of all of my products and services. Make sure to get on my ezine list to receive special offers by sending an email to tips@SellingInfoProducts.com

ORDER SHEET

Product	Price	Qty.	Subtotal
How to Self Publish Your Own Book and Get Famous	$97	____	_____
Marketing and Promoting Your Own Seminar and Workshops	$97	____	_____
How to Make $5,000 a Day as a Professional Speaker	$97	____	_____
Creating and Selling Information Products	$97	____	_____
How to Start and Build a Turbo-Charged Consulting Business	$97	____	_____
24 Direct Marketing Secrets to Your Professional Services Business	$97	____	_____
How to Double Your Sales on the Web in 90 Days or Less	$97	____	_____
How to Get Your Own Radio Show in 7 Days or Less	$97	____	_____
How to Make ANY Product a Best Seller	$97	____	_____
How to Start Your Own Association	$97	____	_____
How to Run Your Own Conferences	$97	____	_____
Writing Effective Web Copy	$97	____	_____
Creating Highly Profitable Joint Ventures	$97	____	_____

Please **CIRCLE** your choices!

Package A: Any 3 items from the list above (and 1 hour of consulting time) $297

Package B: Any 5 items from the list above (and 2 hours of consulting time) $497

Package C: The "whole enchilada" $777

Everything on this list PLUS: 3 hours of one on one consulting (face to face or on the phone); unlimited email assistance; and 50% off any additional products or services

Info Products Bootcamp Audios (close to 24 hours of material) $497

Seminar on Seminars Audios (a full three days of content) $497

TOTAL: Please add $3 per item (per program – not per package) for Shipping . . . . . $ _____

Guarantee: EVERYTHING we sell comes with a no B.S, money back, lifetime guarantee. If you're not happy, SEND IT BACK!

(Please Print)

Name: _____

Company: _____

Address: _____

City: _____ State: _____ Zip: _____

Phone:_____ E-mail:_____

____ VISA ____ MC ____ Amex ____ Enclosed is my check (payable to Fred Gleeck)

Account No.: _____ Expiration Date: _____

Signature: _____

(Charges will appear as Fred Gleeck Productions)

Please send this form along with your check or credit card information to:
Fred Gleeck Productions • 209 Horizon Peak Drive • Henderson, NV 89012
Phone: 800-345-3325 • Fax: 702-617-4278

To collect your free gift (worth $77) send an email to tips@seminarexpert.com

ORDER SHEET

Product	Price	Qty.	Subtotal
How to Self Publish Your Own Book and Get Famous	$97	____	_____
Marketing and Promoting Your Own Seminar and Workshops	$97	____	_____
How to Make $5,000 a Day as a Professional Speaker	$97	____	_____
Creating and Selling Information Products	$97	____	_____
How to Start and Build a Turbo-Charged Consulting Business	$97	____	_____
24 Direct Marketing Secrets to Your Professional Services Business	$97	____	_____
How to Double Your Sales on the Web in 90 Days or Less	$97	____	_____
How to Get Your Own Radio Show in 7 Days or Less	$97	____	_____
How to Make ANY Product a Best Seller	$97	____	_____
How to Start Your Own Association	$97	____	_____
How to Run Your Own Conferences	$97	____	_____
Writing Effective Web Copy	$97	____	_____
Creating Highly Profitable Joint Ventures	$97	____	_____

Please CIRCLE your choices!

Package A: Any 3 items from the list above (and 1 hour of consulting time) $297

Package B: Any 5 items from the list above (and 2 hours of consulting time) $497

Package C: The "whole enchilada" $777

Everything on this list PLUS: 3 hours of one on one consulting (face to face or on the phone); unlimited email assistance; and 50% off any additional products or services

Info Products Bootcamp Audios (close to 24 hours of material) $497

Seminar on Seminars Audios (a full three days of content) $497

TOTAL: Please add $3 per item (per program – not per package) for Shipping . . . . . $ _____

> **Guarantee:** EVERYTHING we sell comes with a no B.S, money back, lifetime guarantee. If you're not happy, SEND IT BACK!

(Please Print)

Name: _____

Company: _____

Address: _____

City: _____ State: _____ Zip: _____

Phone:_____ E-mail:_____

____ VISA ____ MC ____ Amex ____ Enclosed is my check (payable to Fred Gleeck)

Account No.: _____ Expiration Date: _____

Signature: _____

(Charges will appear as Fred Gleeck Productions)

Please send this form along with your check or credit card information to:
Fred Gleeck Productions • 209 Horizon Peak Drive • Henderson, NV 89012
Phone: 800-345-3325 • Fax: 702-617-4278

To collect your free gift (worth $77) send an email to tips@seminarexpert.com

Your Complete Solution to Doing Business on the Web!

www.webmarketingmagic.com

Reasonably priced for all you get and you can pay either monthly or yearly! Try it out for a month for less than $5!

Here's What you get with this amazing program:

E-Book Module: Deliver your digital products including e-books with virtually NO effort.

Shopping Cart: As incredibly easy to use shopping cart even a Mac user like me can figure out!

Client Database System: Keep all your customer records in one place sortable by a variety of fields.

Broadcast Module: Allow you to send out a message to any segment of your database quickly and easily

Smart Auto-Responders: Send people a virtually unlimted nuber of pre-programmed messages.

Forms Module: Create a form for a variety of purposes (including surveys) quickly and easily.

Ad Tracker Module: Track all your advertising by clicks and orders as well as "type-in traffic" to your site.

Coupon Module: Set up and accurately track others who want to sell your products.

Affiliate Module: Create urgency for your offers using either a time elment or a specific number of units.

Tell a Friend Module: Get others to refer people to your site with a few clicks for the mouse.

How do you get started?

Go to www.webmarketingmagic.com and sign up online

Special Offer: Sign up for a full year of webmarketingmagic and get $97 worth of credit towards to purchase of any products of mine being sold for $200 or more.

No matter what you sell, this integrated program will help you to sell more of it! Take a look at some of the incredible features it contains. Also, you can do a 30 day trial for just $3.95. Give it a try!

To collect your free gift (worth $77) send an email to tips@seminarexpert.com

How to Get in Touch with Me

If you need to contact me, the best way to do so is to email me. The best email address for me is fgleeck@aol.com. You can also reach me by calling 702-617-4205. If I'm not at that number my machine will tell you the best number to call to find me.

If you want to mail me something (like a gift for example), feel free to send it to my office in the Las Vegas area at:

Fred Gleeck
209 Horizon Peak Drive
Henderson, NV 89012

Also, if you produce any information products as a result of following my advice, please send me a copy. Preferably, one that's autographed by you.

WARNING!!

On occasion I will get a call from a customer or prospect asking me about a particular product in the information marketing field. I know most of the players in the field and I'm always happy to give you my opinion.

As my "friend" Bill O'Reilly would say, here's the NO SPIN truth: 90% or more of all of the people selling marketing related products are crooks. What do I mean by this? I define a crook as someone who either intentionally defrauds people or someone who delivers much less value than what they promised.

There are some information marketers out there who shade the truth when they promote themselves, their products and their services. There are also others who are downright crooks.

Maybe you can make more money if you are willing to be a sleazy operator - if you're willing to play fast and loose with the facts. BUT, that's not for me. I keep my overhead very low and lead a pretty simple life. The net result? I don't have a huge "nut" to cover every month and don't have to make a sale to put a meal on the table.

I suspect that I'm different than other marketers in this area. When I go out to dinner with a lot of my peers, they want to eat at fancy restaurants and spend lots of cash. That's just not who I am. That doesn't make me any better, it just means that I don't have to pay those massive AMEX bills every month that all of my peers have to do to support a lifestyle like that.

Everyone has to be themselves. You are no exception. But I'll give you my secret for financial success in this business. Keep your overhead low and produce quality products. Then you can do what I do.

So, be careful when you deal with marketers in this field. There are a lot of people who aren't quite on the "up and up."

To collect your free gift (worth $77) send an email to tips@seminarexpert.com

Want to Accelerate The Speed of Your Success?

I have two coaching programs that I've set up for people who want to learn how to "do" this business. One is a program that is geared to those people who want to "do it themselves." The other is geared to those who want to have me "hold their hands on a long term basis."

The do-it-yourself system involves a series of products on topics that are specifically relevant to helping you start and build a successful information product marketing business. Each package is customized to YOU.

Take a look at www.TheProductGuru.com for more information on both of these packages and see which one (if any) is right for you.

I also coach a select number of people each year on how to produce and market their own information products. It is a very expensive program and only for those who are truly serious about this business and willing to spend a lot of time and money to be successful.

It is not a program that you can just pay to get accepted. Not only do you have to have a niche or product line that I believe in, we also have to have a good personality match between us.

To give you the basic structure of the deal, you give me a fee up front and then pay me additional monies from the revenue that I help you start to generate. After you double what you have paid me, I then get a percentage of sales. If you have an interest, the best way to find out more about the program is to go to

But I warn you, the program is expensive and only geared to the truly serious.

If you're interested in either of these programs, call me at 702-617-4206 or go to www.TheProductGuru.com

My $97 GIFT for YOU!

Just for joining my list!

I want to give you something that really is worth $97. Why would I do this? Because I want you to allow me to keep this conversation we've started going. That's right, it's a BRIBE to let me stay in touch with you.

If you're willing to give me your email address I'll send you a transcript of one of my bootcamps that I normally sell for $97. It's yours with no strings attached. If you ever get tired of my sending you information (which I hope NEVER happens), all you have to do is click the UNSUBSCRIBE button that comes with every email that I send out.

I know you already get tons of emails and you hate most of them. This won't be true with what I send you. You'll get a series of great take away information that you can put to use immediately.

To collect your free gift (worth $77) send an email to tips@seminarexpert.com

Fred Gleeck's
Million Dollar Rolodex

(ESSENTIAL CONTACTS YOU'LL NEED – TELL THEM I SENT YOU!)

Contacts you MUST use:

Domain Registration Services: www.UltraCheapDomains.com (LOW prices)

Internet Marketing Consulting: Phil Huff – www.PhilHuff.com

Domain Hosting: www.HostingWithPhil.com

Domain Name/Traffic Generation: Wade Thomas – www.myinternetmarket-ing.com; WadeThomas@aol.com

Legal Matters: David Frees; DMFIII@aol.com; Stephe Soden: 1-619-239-3200

Publicity: Alex Carroll (Alex@RadioPublicity.com) and Paul Hartunian (Paul@Hartunian.com)

Copywriter: Call me for the latest and greatest recommendation

Ghostwriting/Web Copy: Call me for the latest and greatest

Print-on-Demand Printer: Scott Laudenslager; Kimco Printing (303) 295-2574; KimcoPrinting@qwest.net

Book Cover/Interior Designer: Nick Zelinger – (303) 985-4174; www.nzgraphics.com; znick4@qwest.net

Editing: Call me for my latest and greatest recommendation (these are tough to find)

Small Business Accounting: Chris Trinka – 212-628-3139 (in the NYC area only)

Office Products: Viking Office Products – 800-421-1222

Computer Hardware: Mac/Micro Warehouse – 800-622-6222

Computer Software: NUBS (you MUST say you're a Fred Gleeck student); 800-231-6987

Duplicating Machines/Blank Media: Kingdom – www.Kingdom.com; 800-788-1122

Duplication/Fulfillment: Rich Rubinstein

Media Packaging: Sylvia Tapelt - Blackbourne – 888-676-6773

Contact Management Software: Act from Symantec or Filemaker Pro

Time Management Seminar: Franklin Covey – 800-487-1847

Training Technique Seminar: Robert Pike (take ONLY this seminar); 800-383-9120

Credit Card Merchant Accounts: check www.Google.com and put in the key words: cheap merchant account

Data Entry: Deborah (DebData@BellSouth.net) – 888-420-3282

Book You MUST Read:

Influence – Robert Cialdini
Jump Start Your Business Brain – Doug Hall
The Tipping Point – Malcolm Gladwell

Website References You MUST have:

www.WebMarketingMagic.com:
   automated system for doing business online

www.SeminarExpert.com:
   information on how to become a successful seminar promoter

www.SeminarOnSeminars.com
   information on the bi-yearly seminar bootcamp

www.InfoProductsSeminar.com:
   information on the bi-yearly info products bootcamp

www.SelfPublishingSuccess.com:
   site showing how to maximize revenue as a publisher/author

www.ConsultingExpert.com:
   site that shows you how to make money as a consultant

www.TheProductGuru.com:
   site to find out about coaching in the information publishing area

To get yourself on my email list:
Send a blank email to tips@seminarexpert.com

Fred Gleeck • 209 Horizon Peak Drive • Henderson, NV • 89012
800-FGLEECK (345-3325) • fredgleeck@mac.com

To collect your free gift (worth $77) send an email to tips@seminarexpert.com

*A*ppendix B
Sample Forms

Sample Seminar Evaluation

How Would You Rate This Session in Terms of Content? (10 is best)

1   2   3   4   5   6   7   8   9   10

How Would Your Rate This Session in Terms of Presentation? (10 is best)

1   2   3   4   5   6   7   8   9   10

What Did You Like Best About the Session?

_____

_____

_____

What Did You Like Least/What Would You Change?

_____

_____

_____

Additional Comments:

_____

_____

May We Use Your Comments in Our Promotional Material?

If Yes, please sign here: _____

Would you be interested in? (Check if interested):

_____ One on One Coaching

_____ Additional Fred Gleeck Seminars

_____ Monthly Mastermind Meetings

Name: _____

Address: _____

City: _____ State: _____ Zip: _____

Email address: _____

Sample Checklist for Seminars

- ☐ My Promo Material
- ☐ Breakfast items
  - ☐ Tiered Brochure
  - ☐ Profile Sheets
  - ☐ Bus Cards
- ☐ Canvas Bags
- ☐ *Investing for Beginners/Consultants Manual/Negotiate Everything*
- ☐ Order sheets ☐ Handouts
- ☐ Evals ☐ Sign in sheets
- ☐ Name Tags
- ☐ List of attendees with payment records
- ☐ Webmarketingmagic.com stuff
- ☐ Receipts for Credit Card Payments
- ☐ Cash Receipt booklet
- ☐ Product to be sold at the seminar
  - ☐ Tapes
  - ☐ Workbooks
- ☐ Taping Device
- ☐ Freebies Promised if any ☐ Recording Device(s) — audio/video
- ☐ TV/VCR if necessary ☐ Pen/Pencil
- ☐ My books to show people at seminar ☐ Clock
- ☐ My book covers to show points at seminar ☐ Franklin
- ☐ Water to drink
- ☐ Any other promotions to give people
- ☐ Sign in Sheets/Registration Sheets
- ☐ Business Cards: mine and webmarketingmagic.com cards

Sample Hotline Message

(Self-Storage Bootcamp Hotline Message)   (702-617-XXXX)

Thanks for calling about the new and revised one-day self-storage marketing seminar.

If at any point during this message you'd like to speak to someone live and in person, please call my office directly at 800-345-3325.

I don't care what you know about self storage, or how long you've been in the business, you need to take the time to come to this one day event. Whether you own or manage one or 10 facilities. These techniques work.

In one day I'll revolutionize the way you do business. And I guarantee it.

Before I even start to tell you about what you'll learn at this amazing event, let me give you our guarantee.

If you don't make at least 10 times the cost of this seminar in additional profits over the course of the next year, I want you to call me and ask for your money back. If you aren't 100% satisfied, for any reason whatsoever, I want you to take me up on this guarantee.

I am the only one in the storage industry who offers this guarantee. Why is that? I think you can figure it out. The trade shows put on by the various associations don't even offer a guarantee. Why not? Because so much of what they offer is weak. Very weak.

The concepts I'll give you in this one day work. They have been tested with clients around the country for the last 5 years.

If you're looking for a way to spend a relaxing day away from this office, this won't be it. People are usually exhausted by the end of the day. The reason? Because I pack the seminar with information. All meat. No fat. Just lots of easy to use, fully explained tested marketing techniques that are easy to learn and use.

Here's what we're going to cover in this information-packed one-day session.

I'll show you a way to properly design your next yellow page ad. Follow the suggestions I'll give you and you'll get twice or three times as many calls. These are the results my current customers are getting. And you can too. Just follow the step by step instructions I'll give you.

This one section will pay for the cost of the seminar many times over.

If you aren't selling any what I call add on products like boxes and locks, I'll show you how to do it right. Most storage facilities generate 2% of their gross sales from add-on sales. My customers are getting 7 times that much. You'll learn the secrets to putting an additional $5,000 a year in your pocket from this idea alone.

I'll divulge a secret 3 part system to increase your closing ratio over the phone by a minimum of 15%. And I'll show you how to do it in less than 3 minutes. Just think of how much more money you'll make as a result.

I'll show you a way to create an item out of thin air to give away to customers that has as much as $500 of value that will cost you less than a buck. Don't give away free rent. Do what I describe in this section of the seminar.

I'll give you my 4 step program to increase repeat customers by 22% or more. Wouldn't that be nice?

Not using the internet to market your facility? I'll reveal the real story on the internet and it's viability in the storage industry.

I'll also share a simple concept that will increase a customers average length of stay by 50%. Just think how much more money you'd be making if each customer stayed 50% longer.

Referrals are a very low cost marketing method. I'll give you a step by step system to increase them by 30% minimum.

There is so much more that you'll get from this 1 day event, I don't have the time to tell you it all in this brief 4 minute message.

But I guarantee you'll leave with a ton of great, useable ideas. And if I don't, you get every single penny back. How can I do this? Easy. The ideas work.

The problem is that we keep the seminars very small. No more than 25 people. So you'll get plenty of individual attention. So you need to call and register right away. The number to call is 1-800-345-3325.

Can't make it to the seminar? Call the office for a complete set of audio tapes with phone follow up.

Given all the competition in the storage industry, you need to hear this information. And you need to hear it now. Make your facility virtually immune to competition. Register now to attend this 1 day business changing event.

Call 1-800-345-3325 now to register.

I look forward to seeing you there.

To collect your free gift (worth $77) send an email to tips@seminarexpert.com

Speaker Release Form

I, _____ , hereby
grant Fred Gleeck the exclusive rights to the content that I will present at the Publishing Profit Bootcamp in both video and audio form.
It is agreed that Fred will own the copyright to the materials that are
delivered here in Las Vegas, on March 2-4, 2001.

This does not prevent me from delivering the same or similar information at another venue, but the rights and copyright to THIS
presentation (audio and video) for this event belong exclusively to
Fred Gleeck.

If I am selling any products at this event, there is a 50-50 split of the
product sales. If the products sell for $100, Fred Gleeck will receive
50% of the gross sales of the products at this event.

As a speaker at this event, you have the right to sell the videos and
audio tapes at 55% of the list price. You will pay 45% of the list price
+ actual shipping costs. This will be lower than the price we offer any
and all dealers, who normally receive 45-50% off the price of our
products. If you'd like, we will drop ship the audios/videos for you.

Speaker: _____ Date: _____

Fred Gleeck: _____ Date: _____

Bootcamp Schedule

(All times are approximations and are subject to change)

Friday, March 2, 2001

Noon - 1PM . . . . Fred Gleeck

1PM - 2PM . . . . Jerry Jenkins

2:15PM - 2:30PM . . . . Break

2:30PM - 3:30PM . . . . Ted Ciuba

3:30 PM - 4:00PM . . . . Break + Networking Session

4PM - 5PM . . . . Raleigh Pinskey

5PM - 6PM . . . . George Tran

6PM - 6:15PM . . . . Break

615PM - 7PM . . . . Hotseats

(Don't stay out TOO late, remember, we start at 8AM on Saturday)

Saturday, March 3, 2001

8AM - 9AM . . . . Fred Gleeck

9AM - 10:15AM . . . . Kimberly Judd

10:15AM - 10:30AM . . . . . . Break

10:30AM - 11AM . . . . Wade Thomas

11AM - 12 NOON . . . . Tami DePalma

12 NOON - 1:30PM . . . . . . Lunch (On Your Own)

1:30PM - 2:30PM . . . . Claude Diamond

2:30PM - 3:45PM . . . . Yanik Silver

3:45PM - 4:15PM . . . . Break + Networking Session

4:15PM - 5PM . . . . Mystery Guest(s)

5PM - 5:30PM . . . . Mystery Guest(s)

5:30PM - 6PM . . . . George Tran

6:15PM - 6:30PM . . . . Break

6:30PM - 7PM . . . . Fred Gleeck

7PM - 7:30PM . . . . Hotseats

(Remember, 8AM start time on Sunday as well; you DON'T want to miss Alex!)

Sunday, March 4, 2001

8AM - 10AM . . . . Alex Carroll

10:15AM - 10:30AM. . . . . . Break

10:30AM - 11AM . . . . Fred Gleeck

11:00AM - Noon . . . . Hotseats

Sample Individual Speaker Evaluations

Speaker Name: _____

How would you rate the quality of the CONTENT this speaker provided you with? (10 is BEST)

BAD   1   2   3   4   5   6   7   8   9   10   GREAT

How would you rate the quality of the PRESENTATION this speaker delivered (their speaking skills)?

BAD   1   2   3   4   5   6   7   8   9   10   GREAT

What did you like best about this speaker?

_____

What did you like least about the speaker?

_____

Speaker Name: _____

How would you rate the quality of the CONTENT this speaker provided you with? (10 is BEST)

BAD   1   2   3   4   5   6   7   8   9   10   GREAT

How would you rate the quality of the PRESENTATION this speaker delivered (their speaking skills)?

BAD   1   2   3   4   5   6   7   8   9   10   GREAT

What did you like best about this speaker?

_____

What did you like least about the speaker?

_____

Speaker Name: _____

How would you rate the quality of the CONTENT this speaker provided you with? (10 is BEST)

BAD   1   2   3   4   5   6   7   8   9   10   GREAT

How would you rate the quality of the PRESENTATION this speaker delivered (their speaking skills)?

BAD   1   2   3   4   5   6   7   8   9   10   GREAT

What did you like best about this speaker?

_____

_____

What did you like least about this speaker?

_____

_____

Publishing Profit Bootcamp Evaluation

Overall, how would you rate this event?

BAD   1   2   3   4   5   6   7   8   9   10   GREAT

Which speaker(s) did you like best and why?

_____

_____

_____

Which speaker(s) did you find the least beneficial and why?

_____

_____

What comments would you like to give us that we may QUOTE you on? (PLEASE be SPECIFIC)

_____

_____

_____

May We Use Your Comments in Our Promotional Material?

If Yes, please sign here: _____

Would you be interested in? (Check if interested):

_____   One on One Coaching

_____   Additional Fred Gleeck Seminars

_____   Monthly Mastermind Meetings

Name: _____

Address: _____

City: _____ State: _____ Zip: _____

Email address: _____

Registration Information

When & Where: Nov 18th – Los Angeles; Nov 19th – San Francisco; Nov 20th – San Diego; Dec 2nd – Tucson; Dec 3rd –Phoenix; Dec 4th – Albuquerque

All seminars are from 9AM - 4PM

How to Register: You must call or fax to register. Registration is strictly limited to the **first 35** people. This cannot be altered. If the past is any indication of the future, spaces fill up very quickly. If you are interested in attending, call or fax the form on the next page immediately to be assured a space. Don't wait and "do it later."

Guarantee (100% No B.S., Iron Clad, Double Guarantee): I understand that some of you don't know me. That is why I make the following iron-clad double guarantee. If for any reason whatsoever you don't feel like you have received more than your moneys' worth by the lunch break, simply hand in your materials for a complete 100% refund. No weasel clauses, no hassles, no questions asked. In addition to that, if you do not generate an additional $5,000 over the next year as a result of these ideas and concepts, please call me and we will send you a quick and courteous refund. I have never had to give anyone there money back from a seminar in the many years I have been doing them. I think this is because of the incredible amount of **useable** information I pack into such a short period of time.

Early Registration Bonus: The first 5 people to register are entitled to a special free gift worth $99.

Methods of Payment: Visa, Mastercard, or American Express. Check in advance, check at the door (with credit card guarantee) or cash.

Fees: $297 for the first person and $197 for any additional people from the same organization. This includes all seminar materials. Lunch will be provided.

Who Should Not Attend? If you are the type of person who is content to do things the way you always have, this seminar is definitely not for you. If you don't have an open mind or want to learn the latest ideas that have been tested with spectacular results, it would be best **not** to attend.

Comprehensive Workbook: The seminar includes a comprehensive workbook for you to take with you. At the completion of this seminar you will have a complete roadmap for making competition a thing of the past.

A Plan of Action: You will leave this seminar with a comprehensive plan to boost occupancy and ensure long term growth. You will walk out knowing **exactly** what to do next. I will give you a plan, without needing a big bucks budget, to make your competitors' heads spin.

Unable to Attend?: It is always preferable to attend any seminar in person. That way you get your individual concerns and questions answered. However, if it is absolutely impossible for you to make it, call us and we'll arrange for a special price on our "home study" materials. Telephone follow-up is included.

Tax Deductibility: In all likelihood this seminar is tax deductible. Check with your accountant to be sure.

Certificate of Attendance: Everyone who attends the seminar will receive a certificate of completion. Please don't be fooled by various certification programs you see advertised in the industry. The only certification you need are your results and your numbers. I will choose a manager who has taken a facility from 65% occupancy and moved it to 90% in 3 years over any manager with some piece of paper on their wall. The only indicator of how good you are, are your numbers. The numbers don't lie.

Cancellations: If for any reason you have to cancel your reservation, I will refund your money in full if it is more than 48 hours before the seminar. After that time I will give you full credit towards a future seminar, my consulting time, my products, or any combination of those items. Cancellation guidelines are set up to ensure that know one is closed out from attending who wanted to come only to have someone else not show up.

NOTE: Hundreds of people have been exposed to this material and felt it was the most valuable information they have ever heard in the storage business. Check out some of the comments from others. Find out for yourself with absolutely no risk. If you don't agree, you don't pay. Plain and simple.

Seminar Registration Form

3 ways to register: Phone/fax/mail

Phone: 800-345-3325

Fax: 212-996-1884

Self Storage Success® (A division of Fred Gleeck Productions)

317 East 90th St.; Suite 2B

New York, NY 10128

Cities/Dates: Nov 18th – Los Angeles; Nov 19th – San Francisco, Nov 20th – San Diego; Dec 2nd – Tucson, Dec 3rd – Phoenix, Dec 4th – Albuquerque

All seminars are from 9AM - 4PM (sharp — we start and end exactly on time)

Attendance for each seminar is strictly limited — no exceptions, register early!

____ Yes, I/we would like to attend the 51 Secrets of Self Storage Marketing Seminar. Please save me ____ space(s). (Payment <u>must</u> be received to ensure a space).

____ No, I cannot attend, but am interested in the home study materials at a special price.

Fees: $297 for the first attendee, $197 for each additional attendee from the same organization

Total Fees: $ _____ (Please list all who will attend and which seminar they will attend, below)

Method of Payment:

____ **Check:** Please find my check enclosed for $297 (+ $197 per add'l person or seminar) made payable to **Fred Gleeck Productions** (please complete information below)

____ **Credit Card:** Please find the information detailed below.

____ Visa ____ Mastercard ____ Amex

Card Number: _____ Exp: _____

Signature: _____

Name: _____

Company: _____

(Please print name of "primary" attendee or whoever will be paying)

Address: _____

City: _____ **State:** _____ **Zip:** _____

Phone: (   ) _____ - _____

Fax: (   ) _____ - _____

Person(s) Attending:

Name: _____

City: _____

Name: _____

City: _____

Name: _____

City: _____

Name: _____

City: _____

Transcription of My Product Pitch to the
Self Storage Market

Now's time for the 2 minute commercial. Does everyone have an order sheet in front of them?

Good.

Now, let me tell you before we get started that I have been very fortunate over the last few years trading commodities. If you don't buy anything from me here today, I will not miss a meal.

But, if you don't buy the materials, it may have a very significant impact on your finances. The things that I want to talk to you about will have a dramatic effect on your bottom line profits.

There are a lot of items on this list, so I just want to go through each one fairly quickly and tell you what they are all about. Now looking at the order sheet you see the first item. It's a video called Turning Calls Into Visits.

In the storage industry there are 4 steps to success. First, you have to get people to call your facility. That is the marketing side. That's what you are here for today: the first step is getting the phone to ring.

Second, you have to get those who call to come in and visit you. That's where the video Turning Calls into Visits would be great. It will show you specific ways to increase your closing ratio over the phone.

This video also comes with a test to see how well your folks understand and retain the information.

Third, you have to get those who visit to sign on the dotted line to rent a storage unit. This video concentrates on helping managers improve their face to face closing skills. This one also comes with a test.

And lastly, you have to get them to stay forever and tell all of their friends. The two customer service videos are geared to specifically help you in those areas.

30 Days to Better Telephone Technique is a generic telephone skills video. It isn't specific to the storage industry, but it is incredibly helpful. This video will help ensure your people give good service over the phone.

The Add-on Sales Video will help you double or triple your sales of boxes and locks. It is set up to be played when people walk into the office. It's set up to give people tips on storage followed by 24 Quick and Easy Ways to Radically Improve Customer Service is a generic video that will help you improve your overall customer service skills at your business.

Turning Contacts Into Clients is geared to showing you how to generate customers without going the traditional sales route. This video will be very helpful with managers who are going to Chamber of Commerce meetings to show them how to make those meetings really pay off.

In the section where it says Multi Tape Audio Program, the first item in that section is today's seminar on audio. Why buy this program if you came to the seminar? To answer that question, let me first tell you that I have at least 2 clients who buy each new seminar that I tape. Although the outline is the same, the questions from the group are very different. I think you will find it very valuable to have.

Each year we have a marketing bootcamp. This is a very much expanded version of today's seminar over a three day period.

Two cassette audio programs on specific issues include Increasing Your Yellow Page Ad Response by 250%. This expands on the information we've talked about today on designing yellow page ads.

Direct Mail Secrets covers how to substantially increase your direct mail response.

Attracting Highly Profitable Commercial Tenants is a cassette program which will help you target commercial groups. It's worth going after these folks because you will make a lot more money than generic direct mail campaigns that are a waste of your time.

Like we talked about, you need to show people how and why you are different. A USP is essential to this process. And that two-cassette program will show you how.

In addition to everything else you get a one year subscription to the newsletter.

The total for all 8 videos, 22 audio tapes and a newsletter comes to $1074. And that would be a great deal.

BUT, what I'd like to do is have you subtract the cost of today's seminar, which is $297 from that total. If you do, you get a magic number in Las Vegas.

What are you coming up with? $777!

And here's the deal. If you don't make at least 10 times that amount in additional profits over the course of the next year, I want you to send it all back.

To collect your free gift (worth $77) send an email to tips@seminarexpert.com

Please fill out the order sheet and hand it in to me before the end of the day.

And, if you order the "whole enchilada" as I call it, I'll also give you a copy of my new book: "Secrets of Self Storage Marketing Success" which runs over 250 pages. But you can only get the book if you get the big package.

Again, fill out your order sheet before the end of the day. I'll fill the orders on a first come, first served basis.

Now let's go to lunch!

Storage Marketing Seminar Special

(Prices are valid today and today only — no exceptions)

Videos	Regular Price	Seminar Special
Turning Calls Into Visits	$195	$149
Turning Visits Into Contracts	$195	$149
Together as a Package	$295	$195
30 Days to Better Telephone Technique	$149	$99
Customer Service Volume #1	$195	$149
Customer Service Volume #2	$195	$149
Together as a Package	$295	$195
Add-on Sales Video	$99	$79
24 Quick and Easy Ways to Radically Improve Customer Service	$99	$79
Turning Contacts Into Clients without Cold Calling	$99	$79
All of the Above Videos:	$1226	$497

Multi Tape Audio Programs:		
51 Secrets of Self Storage Marketing Success (Today's seminar)	$297	$97
Self Storage Marketing Bootcamp audio tapes (All 12 hours)	$597	$499
Two Above as a Set:	$695	$545

2 Cassette Audio Programs:		
Increase Your Yellow Page Ad Response by 250%	$49	$39
Direct Mail Secrets You Must Know	$49	$39
Attracting Highly Profitable Commercial Tenants	$49	$39
Creating Your USP to Make Yourself Competition-Proof	$49	$39
All Above Bought as a Package:	$149	$99

To collect your free gift (worth $77) send an email to tips@seminarexpert.com

Monthly Marketing Newsletter:

Self Storage Marketing Magic

(10 issues — 1 year subscription) $99 $79

The Whole Enchilada

(22 Audios, 8 Videos + a Newsletter) $2169   **$1074**

(Valid for the next 72 Hours)

Please <u>circle</u> your selection. Your order will be shipped to you shortly (Please Print)

____ **Check:** Enclosed is my check (payable to **Fred Gleeck**)

____ **Credit Card:** Please find the information detailed below.

    ____ Visa   ____ Mastercard   ____ Amex

Card Number: _____ Exp: _____

Signature: _____

Name: _____

Company: _____

Address: _____

City: _____ State: _____ Zip: _____

Phone: (_____) _____ – _____

Please send this form along with your check or credit card information to:

Fred Gleeck Productions

317 East 90th St. Suite 2B, New York, NY 10128

Phone: 800-345-3325 **or Fax:** 212-996-1884

webmarketingmagic.com (Detailed Description)

Shopping Cart

The shopping cart part of this program lets you do e-commerce by creating the function of "add to cart" to your web-site. It also calculates tax, shipping and totals and is hooked into a real time credit authorization system to enable you to get money from your customers. If you don't have an online merchant account you can still take orders and process them off line.

How it is different/better than the alternatives?

Most of the shopping cart systems out there have to be INSTALLED, and configured. You also have to buy your own secured server certificate, which is a very expensive proposition. With this program you need to do none of these things.

All you have to do is to tell the system what you sell and it takes cares of itself. You can literally be up and running in 5 minutes. The Shopping Cart also integrates with a complete client management/marketing system. Others do not. It is also integrated with an affiliate tracking program.

Cost: A program like this on its own? About $1,000.

Client Management System

The client management system stores all of your customers' information in one central database. This enables you to search for a particular clients' history. This also allows you to determine how much total business this customer has done with you and how much they are "worth."

You can see any particular clients previous transactions to make informed decisions about how to treat and or handle them. It would also allow you to make specific offers to clients who may have bought (or not bought) specific products. This can be done quickly and easily.

This client management system also acts very much like a contact manager (ACT or Microsoft Outlook) allowing you to make notes regarding specific clients. You can also import and export clients to and from other databases.

How is this different from other programs?

It is unique because it integrates with a shopping cart and a smart autoresponder and NO ONE else does that. The shopping cart, autoresponder and form all feed into the client management system.

Cost: To program this kind of thing would cost you somewhere around $3,000.

Broadcast Module

Allows you to quickly, easily and cost effectively send broadcasts to your database of customers. Immediately communicate with any group of customers you have created and segmented with one click of the mouse.

How is this different? No other shopping cart system has this valuable function.

Cost: Approximately $1,000.

Smart Auto-Responder Module

This valuable part of the program enables you to send follow up messages to your customers who have expressed an interest in, or have already purchased your products or services.

These messages can be sent as often as you like with no limit to the number you can send. They can also be sent out at any time interval you choose. Using this component of the system will dramatically improve your sales because repetitive timely contact is the key to getting customers to buy from you and buy more often.

How is this program different from others out there on the market? Others charge on a per auto-responder basis. Webmarketingmagic gives you an unlimited number of these auto-responders.

The other advantage of our smart autoresponders is that people are automatically added into your database and become part of your client management system.

Because of the integration with a shopping cart, we are the only company that can automate a post sales, product specific follow up. Set it up once and it's done forever. That is unless you want to change it, which is simple and easy to do.

The reason why this is so amazingly profound is that your ability to sell other products and services to customers depends on how well you can target them with specific offers based on what they have already bought or inquired about from you. NO other system can do this!

The advantage is that you'll sell more products as a result. Why? Because the process of manually doing this is always a nice concept, but few people can do it because of the enormous amount of time and effort involved.

Cost: Depends on how many auto-responders you'd be setting up. The average company would probably pay $60 per month for this service alone.

Forms

Forms are used to capture customer information from those who visit your web-site.

Creating forms has always been a nightmare. Not with webmarket-ingmagic.

Most of the time when you ask your designer to create a form for you their idea is to produce a "form mail" (a form sent via email to you). That's OK if you have a very limited number of leads per day. You could probably manage that in that fashion.

If, however, you have a larger volume of leads per day coming in you'll want to have a system like this to capture the information and put it into a searchable database so that you can send broadcast messages to those who have visited your site.

Why is this different? Very few forms are designed in this manner.

Cost: This would cost you somewhere between $300 and $500.

Ad Tracker

Unlike a system that keeps track of hits and other data about your site, ad tracker tracks the dollar effectiveness of your on-line advertising campaigns.

One of the biggest challenges in advertising is knowing precisely how well something works. This module is the only application that can accurately report revenue generated by your banner advertising.

Other products will give you data as to the number of hits you receive, but in reality that is much less valuable than knowing how many people actually buy from you as a result of a particular banner ad.

This system can be set up in a matter of minutes and requires NO technical knowledge!

How's this Different?: This is the only system in the WORLD that can report campaign specific sales/revenue from a given banner ad.

Cost: If you were to try and get someone to program a system like this for you it would run somewhere between $1500 to $2000.

Affiliate Module

Enables you to recruit hundreds or thousands of other website owners to resell your products for you with the understanding that you will pay them a commission based on their sales.

This is a great way to get free traffic and you will only pay for sales which result. It is simple and easy to set up and administer. Customers can become affiliates within a matter of minutes. No lengthy forms to fill out or questions to answer.

It is easy to use and much more affordable than other similar (although not really) products. It is also the ONLY product out there that is integrated with a shopping cart. You don't have to try and put together systems that weren't meant to work together.

With others this would involve programmers who charge big bucks and you don't know what they are really doing.

Cost: Most programs like this run about $1000.

Coupon Module

This module enables you to create special offers on your site. They are great for creating a sense of urgency and scarcity. This will dramatically improve your sales.

It allows you to make an offer like this on your website: "Between now and the end of the month you get 25% off of any purchase over $100. Hurry! This offer is only good for the first 100 people who take advantage of this offer."

The system will automatically track the number of people who have taken advantage of this offer. It will also prevent anyone from taking advantage of the offer after the expiration date. It will also prohibit anyone from buying after the specific number you set has been reached.

How is this different? It's integrated with the shopping cart. That means you don't have to force a coupon system to work with your shopping cart system. They already "play well together."

This system can also track how many people took advantage of the offer and also the total amount of sales that resulted from this specific coupon offer.

Cost: To create a coupon system like this would run you about $1,000.

Tell a Friend

This feature of the program enables a visitor (either buyer or inquirer) to your website to refer others to your site quickly and easily.

Most people who sell stuff on their sites have a "thank you" screen which appears after an order has been placed. This wastes a tremendous opportunity. Webmarketingmagic will enable you to not only thank your customer for the order, but ask them for a referral. What better time to do it than at the time they have just bought?

This concept is unique. There is no off-the-shelf program that we are aware of that does this extremely important and valuable function.

Cost: If you wanted to get someone to program this for you it would cost you a minimum of around $500.

Fred Gleeck Productions

209 Horizon Peak Drive
Henderson, NV 89012

Dear Speaker:

Thanks for agreeing to speak at the Publishing Profit Bootcamp. Your contribution will be a great addition to the event. I just have a few quick comments to help us make this a great event for all who attend.

1   All speakers will be required to sign a release form before speaking. This form MUST be signed BEFORE you speak.

2   Concentrate your presentation on information that can be **immediately** used and implemented. Give people a clear understanding of not just **WHAT** to do but **HOW** to do it. Keep the presentation logical and easy to follow. Cut out the "war stories" in favor of concise, highly applicable ideas and content.

3   Regardless of how much time you've been given to speak, try and save 10 minutes at the end for Q&A from the audience. This will better serve everyone.

4   Please ask participants to wait for a "Mic Runner" to bring them a mike before letting them ask their question. Just to make sure, please <u>repeat questions</u> from the audience members once asked. Also, **please watch for signals** from the audio/video tapers for signs as to when to **PAUSE** your presentation for tape changes.

5   Please leave us a high quality original of any and all handouts that you use. This will allow us to duplicate them and put them in the materials when we send out to those who purchase the audios and videos. This will only help you to promote yourself and your services to those who listen/watch on tape.

6   **Please** be flexible and understand if things don't work perfectly. It's the nature of the beast. Be prepared to roll with the punches, whatever happens. This could mean your speaking time gets moved or shortened. I apologize in advance for any inconvenience this might cause.

7   Stay around even when you aren't speaking. There will be a lot of great information, but also, the participants may want to ask you questions. Please be available for them. It will only help you in the long run.

8   If you have products to sell, please feel free to pitch them. BUT remember, in order to be successful selling your products, you

have to deliver great content. Talk to me for help in this area. It's my specialty.

9   HAVE FUN! We want to provide you and the attendees with a rich content and an enjoyable experience. You're part of making that process happen!

Thanks Again for Speaking at this Event!

Fred Gleeck Productions
209 Horizon Peak Drive
Henderson, NV 89012
1-800-FGLEECK (345-3325)
fgleeck@aol.com

Dear Publishing Profit Bootcamp Attendee:

Thanks for being here!

You've decided to spend a good deal of time and money to come to this event. I want to make it worth many times what you paid to be here. We have some dynamite speakers who have been instructed to "spill their guts" about everything that they know to help you catapult your business into the stratosphere.

If anything goes wrong during this event, I apologize in advance. We'll do everything we can to make things "perfect" but there are always those things that happen that we have no control over. Sorry.

If you have any questions during the course of the event, please ask Michelle. She'll be your main contact person. Enjoy your free time (which will be limited), but remember, our goal is to give you the best event possible in the time that we have.

In order to give you the maximum value at this event please help us by doing the following:

- When you have a question, please wait for a microphone to come to you so everyone can hear. Also, we'll be audio/video taping this event, so we want to make sure and get your comments on tape.

- We have a jam-packed program. Please be at the sessions ON TIME. They will start ON TIME. If we don't, we won't be able to give you the value for the money.

- Turn all cell phones off so that the group won't be disturbed by the interruptions.

- Many of the people have valuable items that they will make available for you.

- Talk to the speakers at the breaks and "pick their brains" to get maximum value from the bootcamp.

- Network with other people at the event. You'll find all kinds of people who can help you get what you want and vice versa.

Thanks again for attending. I look forward to giving you an amazing educational experience.

lossary

As with any field, the seminar business has a "secret language." It isn't really secret, it just seems that way when you first get started because everything is new to you. This is true of any industry. Those of us who are in the seminar business haven't done this intentionally. It's just worked out that way.

Here are some of the words you'll need to know:

Back end: Any product you sell to people after you've sold them the front end product.

Bootcamp: An extended, multi-day seminar usually with a number of different speakers. (However, a bootcamp can be one day long. Seldom, however, is a single-speaker event a bootcamp.)

Evals: Evaluations that you ask attendees to fill out at your seminar or event.

Front end: The first product that you sell to a given customer.

Hand-held: A microphone that you hold while speaking (the type most singers use if they aren't using headsets).

In-house seminars/On-site seminars: Seminars done for a group of people, all of whom work for or are associated with the same company or association.

Lav: A microphone that is clipped on to a persons tie or lapel. It allows your hands to be free for the presentation.

Product: Anything that you sell to people at or outside your events. This would include, but not be limited to: eBooks, books, CD-ROMs, software, audios, videos, teleseminars, and consulting services.

Seminar: A presentation of whatever length that is fairly one sided with the speaker giving most of the information and the audience sitting and receiving the message.

Venue: The place where you're holding the seminar.

Workshop: A seminar of any length that has an emphasis placed on interactivity.